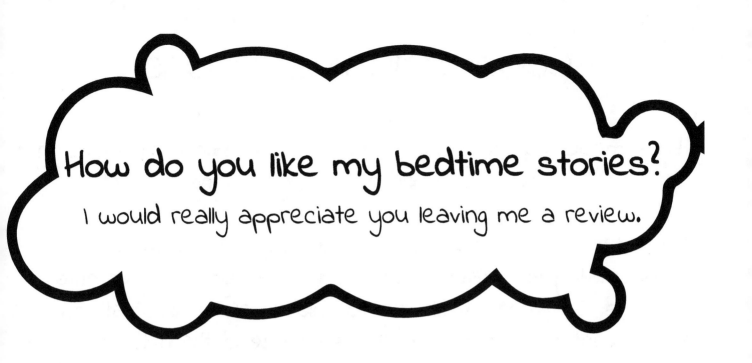

How do you like my bedtime stories?

I would really appreciate you leaving me a review.

Want my additional FREE BONUS PDF bedtime story book?

Like and contact me on my Facebook page:
https://www.facebook.com/Alex-Stone-109388640938614

or scan QR code to get to my Facebook Page:

or send me an email to get your free bonus PDF bedtime story book at:
alexstonebooks@gmail.com

Coloring My Illustrations

I have made my story book with 80 handdrawn illustrations that you or your kid can enjoy coloring in.

I wanted to make this book interactive and creative with the possibility to create the characters as you or your child envisions. So please feel free to color in all the illustrations and if you want to even take pictures and send them to me. I love seeing creative art with my stories. I am always easily reachable on my Facebook page. (Link in beginning of book)

I recommend using color pencils or crayons as they do not bleed through the page.

Use this page as your pencil and pen testing page to see how the bleed through is and how the colors come out for coloring my illustrations.

Stories by Alex Stone

want my additional **FREE BONUS PDF** bedtime story book?

Like and contact me on my Facebook page:
https://www.facebook.com/Alex-Stone-109388640938614
or scan QR code to get to my Facebook Page:

or send me an email to get your free bonus PDF bedtime story book
at: alexstonebooks@gmail.com

Special Wish Lists

Every year Santa gets millions of wishes on children's Christmas Lists. Many of those are very reasonable, they make sense and they are easy to fill. A child who has been behaving well for a long time wants a new bicycle, easy. A girl who has always been doing well at school wants a toy oven to play with, no problem, the elves have plenty of those in stock. A boy who has been keeping up on all the chores wants an Ice Cream Cone Maker, Anytime, the Elves love building those.

However every year, there are some children, usually, the younger ones, that don't know how hard or impossible it would be for Santa to actually fulfill some of their wishes. You see it's not a problem to fill a $20 Gift Card order, but if a child puts in a wish for a million dollars, well. Another example, a child may want a dolphin plush toy, no problem, but another child may want an actual real dolphin, well... Or a child may want a toy tractor, but to ask for a real tractor, well...

Santa realizes the life of a child may be hard and he or she may be building up their ability to be a part of the real world through the world of toys, but sometimes children are ready to just jump into it so fast without knowing the consequences. It would be easy if he could just have a discussion with the parents, but then the parents would know what they asked Santa for Christmas, and we can't always let that secret out can we?

So sometimes Santa has trouble. But there are some times where the child has been so incredibly good and helpful all year long, that even though the wish list is a little on the crazy side, the list does not get filed into the impossible section, it gets filed into the special wishes section.

Wishing to meet Santa can usually be handled by having one of his doubles, trained by Santa meeting the child, or by having himself come out to meet the child at the mall, but a special wish to meet a famous athlete or musician, well that's not so easy.

To qualify for the special wish list, a child would need to meet two very important qualifications. Number one, they have to have been incredibly, astoundingly, and astonishingly good. They would have to be beyond good, helpful, caring, loving, etc. And number two, their wish, while practically impossible, would have to have some small chance of being filled even if very very unlikely, it would at least have to be physically possible.

Now just to put it into perspective, every year, Santa receives one and a half billion wish lists, of these about fifty thousand fall into the absolutely impossible lists section, and of those only about ten fall into the special wishes list section.

When a special wish arrives at the North Pole, Santa gets an immediate alert and would go over the request with the elves directly to see what could be done.

Today was one of those days. A special request had just arrived in the North Pole for a young boy named Henry. Henry was a young boy of seven, and his request met both qualifications. Number one, he was astonishingly, incredibly good. Henry's father you see, served in the military and worked halfway across the world in a country called Iraq. Henry would never see his father for years, and he lived on a farm. Henry was very sad that he could hardly ever talk to his father only online once every three months, but rather than complaining about never seeing him, he learned how to use some of the smaller safer equipment, he learned how to work with some of the smaller safer animals and he learned how to feed all the livestock.

It was a big job, normally the job of an adult, but he did it anyways. One time he even scared off someone who looked like he wanted to steal something with a cowbell. He was a boy alone and had grown up too fast. But his contribution to his family and to his mother was astronomical. At the age of seven, he had already become the man of the house.

number two, his wish, although practically impossible, was somehow very very remotely doable. One could at least imagine how it could be done, Santa read Henry's wish list out to the gathered elves to see what they thought. It did not take long, because his list was very short, he only had one wish, "Dear Santa, Thank you for making every Christmas so special. You have given me everything I ever asked for, you are the best! But this year I really only want one single thing. If you could grant me this wish, I promise I will be the best boy you have ever seen and I will make you prouder than any other boy in the world. This year I just want to see my father one time and play catch with him. That's all I want. Then he can go right back to protecting the world with his bravery. Thank you Santa, I know you can make this happen. You are the best."

The elves, looked at each other and then at Santa. They were teary eyed. Such a deserving boy, and really such a simple request. They looked up to Santa."Well, what do you think my children?", said Santa, "Is it possible?"

The elves thought about it and said, "We just don't know. Protecting the world is such an important job, we can't just take his father away from it even if it is for just a short time. Do we know what he does in the army?"

They went to do some research. It looked like he was in charge of an entire group of aircraft which helps protect the area by watching who is moving where and doing what. It was an important job.

"Is there anyone who could take his place, for just one day? Is there anyone qualified at all?"

It didn't look like it. The father, a Sergeant Major Anthony Tompkins was in charge of a fleet of five hundred aircraft, watching over an area of five thousand square miles. It was a big deal, and very important.

"Maybe we can just arrange for them to have a video call like they did last year." suggested one of the elves.

"No no no, that won't do at all," said Santa, "That's just what they did last year and that's also not what he asked for. He is very very deserving. There has to be someone who can replace him."

They looked and looked and looked and there was no one.

Santa thought about it for a while along with the elves. After a great while, he got up from his chair and walked over to the telephone. He got ready to make a phone call...

* * *

It was Christmas Morning and Henry and his mother were getting ready to have breakfast. Henry had already set the table and gotten everything ready while his mother did the cooking. He even set the table to include his father in the chance that he might make it to the table for once, he hadn't been home for three years. He even had the baseball and gloves ready to go in the backyard.

But Henry's mother knew that he probably wouldn't make it. She had even asked Anthony, and she knew he couldn't, but she didn't want to break Henry's heart. She couldn't bear to disappoint him again.

They sat down and got ready to eat when they heard a voice from outside, "Hey wait up for me!"

Someone was racing towards the front door. It was Anthony, Henry's father!
He burst through the door and spread his arms. His wife and child flew into him with full force
and they hugged and hugged while fighting back tears of happiness.

They had breakfast together. They played catch together. They had lunch together, a picnic. They
talked about farming together. They played basketball together. They
had dinner together. It was the best day of their lives. They got so lost
in the day together, that before he had to go back on a plane again,
it only then occurred to Henry's mother to ask how it was that he was
able to make it home for the day? She thought he was irreplaceable.

Anthony replied, " A very strange thing
happened. The Commanding Office of the
entire United States Air Force called me
and said I could come to see you guys.
He said that for one day my job would
be covered by a flight squad named
R. Deere under the command of an
officer named S. Klosse. Never
heard of him, have you?"

It was the very First Christmas

A very strange book was found in the dusty back area of the North Pole one year, it
was a bit hard to read, both because it was so old, and also because it seemed to use
a version of English that hadn't been used for a very long time. But the elves found it
interesting nonetheless. It was called the Very First Christmas. They read through it.

It seemed that when the world had first learned of Christ and his gift to mankind many others
also wanted to pass on his knowledge. But with many traditions and wonderful practices yet
to be learned one young boy took it upon himself to spread the joy of giving to the rest of
the world by himself. He saw the love that Christ had given to others the world over, and he
wanted to pass on some of that love himself.

This included all children young or old, white or black, girls or boys. Everyone could use some
cheering up. No one was going to get left out.

He learned some very important lessons from Christ, he learned that sometimes it's better to give than to receive, and sometimes it's better to give love, than to need it in return. This boy was a very special boy because he learned all the right lessons. His name was Nick Klosse. But his father liked to call him Nicolas.

He was a boy who looked into the future of the world and what he saw was that the children of the world would eventually be the adults of the world and that they were important. It was the children that were still growing and learning, he decided, that he wanted to help the most, because if no one helped them now, what kind of future would the world be in later? The children of the world, after all, would inherit the Earth.

He went around and asked the children, what is it they want the most? Is there something that you like? He must've talked to a hundred young children to get their opinions and he found one by one they all had different desires. One wanted a toy doll, another wanted a toy sword, another wanted a ball. But it was becoming more and more apparent to him that what they wanted were small things, playful things, and happy things. If it could be summed up into one word, they just wanted toys.

Well, that was easy enough. He was a boy himself, he loved toys too. So if he could provide them with toys, that was a great way to show them that they were loved by someone and that they really mattered. He was overjoyed at the thought of giving them exactly what they wanted and started planning how he would do it. Maybe he could find a toymaker.

But, should he give them a new toy every single day? That would be very hard, and a lot of work. Plus it would not be special then. He had to think of a day, maybe just one day, where children could be held as special and that children could also look forward to. Let's see, maybe just one day of the year, but which day? Hmmm, how about the Birthday of that one very special person who taught him all the great values of living, maybe the Birthday of Christ was that day, and so December 25th, was born.

-5-

He went around town and found someone who was a toymaker. He would have to prepare for that day by getting together as many toys as he could so that he could get them out to all the children. He had come up with the idea for Christmas in September, and so he only had a few months to prepare everything. He worked around the clock, and with the help of the toymaker, that year he was able to make twenty toys. It wasn't enough and he knew he needed help, so he would have to find a group of people willing to help children, just like him, and work for free.

He lived up north where it was cold and the town he was in had about a hundred and twenty children. He didn't quite know how to announce what he called a celebration of Christ by just yelling in the streets, so he decided the best way to draw attention to himself, was to go to the very center of town and decorate a big tree as much as possible. They didn't have lights in those days, so being very careful, Nick lit candles all around so people would notice, and in the tree, he put little figurines. It was definitely weird and different but people came out. To make everyone in town notice him, he put a bright candle with a star on the very top, and so the Christmas tree was born.

Little Nicky, yelled that he wanted to celebrate the future of the world, he wanted to celebrate the children, and that he had free toys to give out. He had a bag of toys that he and the toymaker had made over those four months and anyone that arrived with their kids, got a free toy. His only exchange was seeing the smiling faces of the children that he helped that day. It was all he ever wanted. And so the spirit of giving was born.

But there were so many more children than he had presents, he was short by a lot. So next year he had to think of something. Also, not every family came out to see what was going on, there were only about thirty or forty families that came out. Next year he would have to go out to them. He had to think of a way to get to them quickly and easily in the snow. This was long before there were cars, but they did have sleds, he just needed a bigger one, and so the Christmas Sleigh was born.

The next year, he spent all his time making toys so all the children of the village could have one, and for the ones that didn't come to the tree, he would go to them. There were so many children and so many toys, he had to p u t them in boxes so they would fit in the bag. It was always a mystery what the next would get, and so the idea of presents was born.

This was so exciting to the children and it really made them so happy and so cared for that the idea quickly spread to the next nearby town and the next and the next. Everyone wanted to be part of this. Free toys? Are you kidding me, this is the best thing ever! Let's bring this everywhere!

The boy really wanted to bring Christ to all the masses of people of the world, he didn't want to leave anyone out. He wanted Christ for the masses, and so the word Christ-Mass or 'Christmas' was born.

When someone is so helpful to all mankind that his actions can never be forgotten and his actions are even considered miraculous through his or her spreading of love to everyone around them, then we eventually remember them by referring to them as a Saint. Christmas had finally spread to the far corners of the world and Nick was honored with the title of being a true Saint.

He would grow older but his mother would always refer to him as the Saint, or "Sainty" as she liked to say, and by others, he would be called Old Nicolas. He would live for thousands of years learning to give Christmas to more and more each year, eventually reaching millions of kids. But you know over time words sometimes change around and the name Sainty, of course, became Santa. His last name also got changed around too from Klosse, and he would be known as Claus, and so the name Santa Claus was born.

The elves LOVED the book and couldn't wait to show Santa what they found after they read it. They rushed it over to him and told him to read it.

"Oh, that's where it is! I've been looking all over for that! Thank you for returning it to me, my children," said Santa, "I will keep it safe in a special place this time never to lose it again, Ho ho ho! Thank you thank you thank you!"

Even Superheroes Have Christmas

Mr. Miracle was his name, and being a superhero was his game. There are many different kinds of superheroes out there you know. Each with their own special powers. Some have super strength, some could see through walls, some could fly. Some could shoot an arrow from a mile away and still hit the bullseye. Some had only one power, but some could fly, be invisible, and carry buildings, all three!

Mr. Miracle was a special kind of superhero because while many other heroes had one ability or two or three, he seemed to have all abilities. He could fly, he could breathe underwater, he could bend steel, see through walls, create fire, slow time, you name it he could do it. He could even create objects out of thin air. Not to mention making extremely entertaining TikTok videos. He was a very good-hearted fellow, so he never broke any laws by creating money out of thin air or anything else that was dangerous. And over his time he had saved many many lives from the clutches of his evil nemesis, Mr. Below-Average Maker.

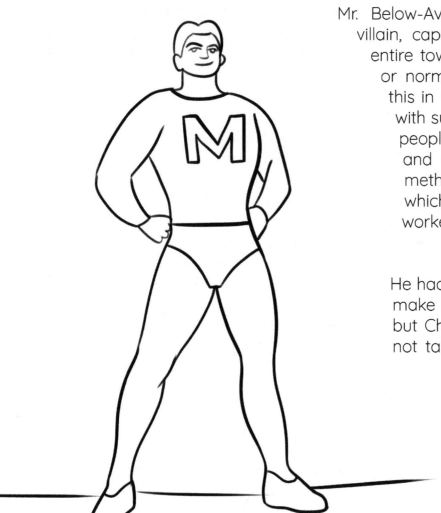

Mr. Below-Average Maker was a very powerful villain, capable of changing entire villages, No, entire towns, NO entire cities, from being great or normal, into being below average. He did this in various different ways, he used candy with super high amounts of sugar that made people get a sugar rush and then get tired and worn out, or he used other very evil methods, like making How To videos online which didn't actually make anything that worked, causing thousands of people to waste their time.

He had many plans and plots in the works to make his next town into well below average, but Christmas was coming along. Would he not take a break from his evil schemes, or would he celebrate? Mr. Miracle was hovering just outside his enemies base by the top window, keeping a careful watch over him to make sure that he didn't try anything funny to ruin people's Christmas.

He used his super-hearing to listen to every word Mr. Below-Average Maker said so he could stay on top of his plans. It looked like he was talking to one of his henchmen.

"Are they ready yet Hugo? We need as many as we can get?"

His henchman, Hugo, who seemed to be very obedient, was quick to answer, "Yes, master. The toys are ready."

"Excellent, excellent, and are they average?"

"No, master. No, not at all, they are far far below average. In fact, they have a battery life which lasts only twenty minutes, if even that."

"Excellent, excellent, and are they fun?"

"No no no master," replied Hugo, "They are fun, but only for about one minute, then they quickly become boring and repetitive."

"Excellent, excellent, and finally, tell me, are the toys durable, will they last or will they break apart after the first playing."

"Oh definitely, they are designed to break on the second time they are used. We used the cheapest plastic we could find."

"Excellent, then my plan is working out perfectly. This Christmas will be the most below average Christmas anyone has ever heard of. Excellent toys and games will be replaced with our toys. The wrapping will be the same and no one will ever know it was us. Pretty soon, all the children in the entire town will get disappointed in Christmas and then we will move onto Phase Two: The Below Averaging of Easter, We're going to make eggs that are just eggs, with no chocolate in sight! Hahahahahahahahahaaaaaaaaaaa!!!!"

Mr. Miracle took careful note of his plans and made plans of his own. There was no way he would allow anyone to have an average Christmas, much less a below-average Christmas. Not on his watch. He carefully observed as the toys rolled off the assembly lines, there were thousands of them. He waited until they were ready to be put into wrapping paper before he made his move.

But while Mr. Below-Average Maker had his ideas of Christmas, Mr. Miracle had some ideas he was going to put into motion. Last Christmas, it appeared that Santa had forgotten Mr. Miracle, for he didn't get any present of any kind. Which meant that Santa probably believed that he already had everything he could ever want. Which was true, anytime Mr. Miracle wanted something, he just made it. Unless it was one of those absolutely delicious egg rolls from his favorite Sushi restaurant Wok'n Roll. Those he had to buy.

But that being the case it also meant something else. If HE didn't get anything for Christmas, well then, Mr. Below-Average Maker probably didn't get anything for Christmas either. After all, he was constantly being bad. But no wonder he was so grumpy, he thought.

But he had a plan. He had prepared everything already, and with tomorrow being Christmas, his plan was ready to be put into motion. He got ready to fly away, but just before he did, he used his superpowers to slow down time, then he used his super strength to break into the evil hideout, and then he used his super-speed to get to each of the three thousand four hundred and fifty toys.

For each and every toy he used his electricity to charge the battery to last for months, then he used his great intelligence to add a computer circuit to make each toy unpredictable and fun, and then he used his heat ray to make the toys almost indestructible. The children would love them. And then with his super-speed he disappeared as fast as he had appeared with no one the wiser. The henchman began wrapping the toys. But just before he left, he left behind a certain something by Mr. Below-Average Makers tree and was gone!

When Christmas arrived Mr. Below-Average Maker noticed that there was actually a present by his tree. Amazed, since he never got anything before he went over to it and carefully picked it up, in case it was some kind of weapon or bomb. He held it up and shook it, hmmm, it seemed all right. He had it X-Rayed and scanned and it checked out as not being dangerous. He opened it, it was a scrapbook!

In it were all the newspaper clippings of his battles with Mr. Miracle. There were notes on some of the fights like, "Hey, you almost got me on that one." and "This was a really great move by you."

He looked through it all and re-lived all the memories he had fighting Mr. Miracle. After he was done, he saw that the present had a card to it. He read it:

To: Mr. Below-Average Maker
From: Mr. Miracle

Thank you for being the best arch-nemesis a guy could ever ask for. It is because of you that my life is so much more interesting and fun. I hope that you have a far above average Christmas and here's to many more battles. Your buddy, Mr. Miracle.

In another part of the town, Mr. Miracle had gotten a present of his own. Seeing it was from Mr. Below-Average Maker, he also had to make sure it wasn't a bomb or a weapon. Then he opened it. It was a Gift Card to Wok'n Roll, now he could get lots of egg rolls and not have to worry about paying for them. What a perfect present!

And for one day, instead of battling to the death, they each had a friend.
Merry Christmas

Wrapping Paper Blues

We've all had the experience, we start wrapping a present and are using our favorite wrapping paper. We wrap and wrap and are angling the present properly, only to find that we've run out of our favorite paper. It's hard sometimes to do the perfect job of wrapping, that's why many times we leave all the wrapping to the elves in the North Pole. They really know what they're doing up there.

In fact, of the many jobs that there are for Christmas, wrapping was not just another job like any other. There were so many ways of wrapping a present it was almost too hard to count. Some presents didn't even come in a box, they were in a bag with tissue paper and the right amount of ribbons. The ribbons themselves had to be styled so as to curl the exact right amount. And color selection! Don't even get me started with color selection. In order to have a beautiful scene under the tree, you could have a red and green present, but you also had to balance it out with blues, yellows, oranges, and really all the colors of the rainbow. In some cases, it had to match the tree. This is not to mention that there are shiny colors as well as designs in the paper, like silver and gold, and also bows that come multi-colored. So the truth is, if you really want to work in the toy workshop wrapping department at the North Pole you had to have passed the Advanced Elf University with flying colors and gotten a top score in Art and Design.

Millions of presents had to be wrapped quickly and perfectly and beautifully, and they had to match and fit with the home. In the North Pole, there were only fifteen elves who measured up to the qualifications to be able to keep up. Of these fifteen, one elf, Shimmy, was their boss and made sure that everything was rolling along as it should.

The wrapping department, while super important, was not an area however that Santa visited very often you see because Shimmy did such an excellent job each year, Santa never had a need to oversee it. Year after year after Shimmy always made sure they had thousands of different kinds of paper, millions of ribbons, boxes, and on and on.

But Shimmy had now been doing this for about one thousand years and Elves, you see, don't live forever. Shimmy was starting to make the tiniest of mistakes here and there, and also had a bit of a harder time seeing. Nevertheless, Shimmy, being who she was, would NEVER admit that she had ever made a mistake, and questioning her or her actions never worked out too well. Shimmy could get angry.

No one had the strength to tell her that it might be time to retire and rest up for a bit and train someone to take her spot. This was a natural part of life, and you couldn't continue to do something forever, thought the elves.

But this year was rolling along, the elves even made sure that they had extra paper, above and beyond what they normally would need in case anything did happen to go wrong. Everything was going totally fine. There was no problem at all. All year round they prepared the paper and the ribbons and material and wrapping would begin as early as September for some parts of the world where children knew what they wanted already. But then it happened...

Shimmy slept in and didn't show up for duty. This wasn't too big of a problem. The rest of the elves stepped up and while figuring out the right wrapping paper was sometimes difficult without her calling the shots, they managed. But they did start to fall behind a little. When Shimmy did finally show up, they caught up again, but not fully, and not everything matched.

Shimmy was quite upset at the elves for letting things slip, but also at herself for sleeping in. But it was OK, she would never let that happen again.

They had to work extra hard and over the course of a week, they were all caught up again. It was still September after all. They had plenty of time. But then it happened again, Shimmy slept in and arrived late. She was One thousand one hundred and eleven years old after all. She probably needed it. The elves worked and worked and worked to keep up with the wrapping and did their best to make everything match and to keep up with the flow of toys. Wrapping millions of presents is quite a job and it would become very intense in December. They would all have deadlines to complete, to make sure Santa had everything he needed before he took flight.
But they fell behind again. Poor Shimmy slept in the next day as well, and the elves really fell behind. They tried their best to keep up, but no one knew wrapping and matching as good as Shimmy and they really needed her. They were now full a day behind. If they didn't catch up then come Christmas, Santa would enter his sleigh with millions of completely unwrapped presents spoiling the surprise. We couldn't have that.

It was that night that the fourteen remaining elves called an emergency meeting with Santa, but without Shimmy there, she had already wandered off to bed, to see what they could do.

Jiminy was the first to say, "We just need to hire more elves! Fourteen of us is not enough, we are already working as hard as we possibly can and with more and more children in this growing world each year, we just can't keep up!"

"Yes, but only Shimmy knows how to wrap presents best. She is our guidance, without her leading us we are lost. There is no one that can do what she does. She is irreplaceable. We are doomed." said Farly the Elf.

"What do you think we should do Santa? Shimmy is too proud and she would never let anyone replace her or even teach another how to do what she does? And yet we are falling further and further behind. We won't be ready by Christmas!"

Santa listened and looked a bit sad. He thought it over and said, "Well, my children. I have known Shimmy for a very very long time. Why don't you let me talk to her."

* * *

The next morning, Shimmy was getting ready to get to work when she realized she was falling behind again. She looked at her alarm clock and found that it had already gone off, she just didn't hear it again. She rushed out of the stocking bed and got her socks on. Then raced over to turn the alarm clock off, only to find someone had already turned it off for her. It was Santa Claus himself.

"Good morning Shimmy, how are you feeling?" he said.

"Oh, not good. If I don't get to work soon we'll fall even further behind! I have to go, I'm sorry." and Shimmy tried to push Santa aside. But Santa stood strong.

"Ho ho ho! No no, my friend, it's been so long since we talked. How long has it been, a hundred years? You've done your job so well and for so long, I have never even thought about the wrapping department in forever. You have been doing perfectly, my dearest dearest friend. But I think it's time you and I talked, what do you think?" Santa said with a caring and loving smile.

"You know Shimmy, it is true, no one could do your job as well as you can. You are a true master. But all people eventually have to pass on their knowledge so that others may follow in their footsteps. It is in this way, your legacy and your love for mankind will live on in others forever. You will never be forgotten in time because what you pass on will be what guides the next generation in their actions. It is in fact the greatest honor you could give me, and it is the greatest honor you could ever bestow upon the children of the world."

Shimmy, didn't say anything, she only looked on. She was speechless.

"I never told you this Shimmy, but you are actually one of my most favorite people in the whole world. I know I can always depend on you. Now, I may ask a huge favor of you. Will you pass on your knowledge to your friends? Will you help pass on your light to the next bright and willing soul so we can keep your light shining into eternity?" Santa looked at her with a loving smile.

Shimmy, looked down at her hands, they were wrinkled, it was true. And while she no longer had the ability to use her body so well, she did have the knowledge, the tremendous knowledge of how to always do her job and do it well, but she just couldn't keep up physically anymore. Maybe Santa was right. She looked up at him with a small tear in her eye, "I will."

And so it came to pass, Shimmy chose her brightest and most hardworking elf, Jiminy, and taught him everything she knew. She poured all her heart and all her love into her teachings and made sure he knew how to do his job absolutely perfectly. She did this for the next few years until Jiminy could finally do it without any further help. And because she passed on her knowledge, Shimmy's love of children and of people the world over would live on in the work of the elves forever and until the end of time.

The Ultimate Present

Young James was a little different from the other children in his class. You see, while the other children were playing games with cards or playing games on their phone, young Mister James was more concerned with stocks and bonds and business matters. There was absolutely nothing wrong with playing and having fun, these things just weren't fun for James.

James liked games as well, in fact, he loved them, but he was very very mature and knew that as he grew older, he would gain more and more responsibility and one of those responsibilities was to make sure that sure he had a good income or a good business and could look after his family and children of his own if he had them in the future.

This was very different, so different, in fact, that sometimes the other kids would make fun of him. But he didn't care so much. He was thinking in futures, not the right now, and while they may make fun of him in school now when he grew up and had things in place in the right way, he would be so successful that, for other kids to make fun of him now, would only drive him to succeed even more. He even WANTED some of the kids to make fun of him every now and then. It could be part of his story.

James was very good at math. He knew that if he started saving money at an early age, and this money gave him a normal amount of interest then in twenty years or so he would have doubled his money, and the more money he saved the more he would have in the future in order to live a successful life with. And he loved to read and he loved to study. He spent his free time learning. He played a little but no so much.

In studying, he learned that if he was going to start a business, he would have to work hard at it. But if he was going to work hard at it then it would have to be something he would have to love to do and that this was very important. He researched what types of businesses he could start, he wasn't sure. He could become an athlete, but he wasn't that good at sports and he didn't have such a deep love of it.

He thought that in order for him to start a business, he would need a loan. Then he got it! He would ask Santa for the loan! He started writing his wish. He thought it might help to keep it simple and only have one thing on it, since if he got this one thing, then eventually if he succeeded he would be able to buy himself anything he wanted anyways. In his wish list, he asked Santa if he could have a million dollars to start his business. He just didn't know what he wanted to do just yet.

* * *

As Christmas time drew near, through some strange twist of fate, James' father, Joseph Cartwright Sr, somehow got a hold of his Christmas wish list. He was always very proud of James and he was interested to read what he wanted, he was always very busy in his own business that he rarely had time to spend with his son. But he loved him very much. Every once in awhile, he would spot little James staring at him when he wasn't watching. What was he thinking during those times? Oh well, let's take a look.

Oh wow! A million dollar loan for a business! Hahahaha! Well, that may be too much for a boy of eight to manage. What would he do with it? Does he even know what kind of business he wants to start? Well, maybe we could make this Christmas special nonetheless.

Christmas morning had arrived and although James had still not quite figured out what he wanted to do with his life, presents were waiting for him under the tree. His father was a great provider after all. Let's see if he got that loan.

Joseph Senior sat nearby and watched them as he opened them one by one.

The first present that James got was a bundle of books on how to find and start a new business that interested James very much. He was sure to read all of them.

His father was starting to learn something about his son that he never knew before as he watched him open more presents.

The next present James opened was a checkbook. His father was happy to explain to him that they had opened a savings account for him that he could use when he was eighteen and that any money he put into it would gain interest and the more he put in the more he would get out when he became older. Again very very exciting!

His father looked on and something was starting to become very apparent to him now.

James opened his next gift and his eyes lit up. It was a board game involving buying and selling properties and also had to do with business. It was a game a son and father could play together. James was so happy, even though there was no million dollar loan in his presents.

Now his father had a handle on it, he watched his son more and had figured it out. When his son was stealing looks at him while he was in a business meeting or on the phone, those looks he was getting were looks of admiration and envy. His son wanted to learn business and finance not because he really had love or understanding of them. His son wanted to be like his father.

Joseph Sr walked over to his son and gave him a big hug. "Hey son, I think I've been neglecting you haven't I? We have barely spent enough time together over the last few years." He started to cry, "You know I love you, son, I have just been working so hard so that you would be able to have everything you ever wanted. But I completely forgot that in working all the time I have not made any time for you, even though making you happy is practically all I live for. Do you see that board game?" He pointed to his present, "Well, that is something we are going to play together regularly ok? And from now on you can be in on my meetings and I will take you to work so you can learn all about business if you want."

"But you know, he said, sometimes it's ok to be a kid too. Make sure to spend time with your friends at school too. A happy life has a balance, and I think we both have been too involved in business that we completely forgot about other parts of our lives. Let's never do that again, ok?"

And so it was. Father and son started playing board games together, they would go on fishing trips together and spending time for real together. James also started playing with his friends in school more rather than focusing all his attention on being like his father. He became much much happier as a result. And finally, rather than getting a check for a million dollars, because his father taught him everything he knew about business over the years, young James, grew up and received the knowledge of how to make his own million dollars many times over in his adult life. It was the best Christmas ever!

A Fairy's Protection

Have you ever had a moment in your life where you thought something terrible was just about to happen and it didn't? Have you ever had a time where you were scared and there was something dangerous near you, or you could've gotten harmed, but you ended up completely fine? Well, it is quite possible, my friend, that you are not the only one. Many people have had such an experience.

Today I am going to let you in on a little secret. You see, surviving those very dangerous situations may not have been by accident. There are a very few, but very powerful tiny little creatures in this world that protect us. There are only about two hundred of them. But they look after us when we don't look after ourselves. We call them fairies and they are a very important part of Christmas.

The next time you find yourself skipping ahead for no reason on the street only to look back at the speeding car that was in the spot you would have been, it may not have been completely you. It's just quite possible that a loving little someone might have given you a push. Or the next time you decide not to step into a ditch that had a pitfall in it, it may not quite have been your decision, someone may have been looking out for you. Did you really make the choice not to drink the sour milk? Or did you have a little help?

Yes, fairies have been with us for thousands of generations, but we never see them. They are very small. But that doesn't mean they are weak or that their hearts are small. For their hearts and their love of man, may just be the strongest of all.

Maybe we all have our little fairy protectors. Maybe everyone does, even the elves in the North Pole! Maybe even Santa has his own protection.

It was the middle of the year and things were slow in the North Pole. Not too much goes on during July as no one is thinking of Christmas. It is hot outside and there is no snow. Summer vacations and summer fun are far more important. And it is this time that Santa sometimes lets his guard down and rests up a bit. Thankfully, should anything ever happen, fairies have a reaction time five times as fast as a normal human and can often predict things before they happen. Without their magic, who knows where we would be.

Santa was just finished sipping on his fruit punch when he made his way across the toy warehouse. The elves had finished making a new batch of toys in the teenager section. These were bigger toys that sometimes had motors or heavier machinery. Bigger kids like bigger things, you know. But it seemed like an average day, nothing special was happening. The only difference was that because there was no real rush or urgency, some of the elves had gotten a little sloppy when stacking the giant boxes of toys. Santa was making his way through the warehouse with boxes stacked on boxes stacked on more boxes and more boxes. And they were heavy.

But Santa wasn't worried, nothing had ever happened to him. It was impossible for him to get hurt anyways, he thought.

It was at that moment that it happened. A little fairy by the name of Lorelei was nearby and could feel something was about to happen. She was a very tiny fairy, small even by fairy standards. But she sensed there was something wrong. Santa was about to walk between some very dangerous and heavy boxes and they could fall on him at any second. She got very alert and watched him carefully to make sure he would be safe.

High above there was a box holding a moped that had come loose. She had to find a way to make Santa walk in another direction for just a second and he would be fine. She had to think fast because Santa was just too big and heavy to move. Like lightning, she sprang into action. She found a mirror and using her fairy super-speed she flew ahead of Santa and reflected some light.

For just a short moment Santa was blinded and stopped walking!

Perfect! Thought little Lorelei. This would save his life! She watched as the box fell, it was like slow motion to her, but to you and me it was in real-time. Then the unthinkable happened. The falling box fell onto another box which then fell into another box. Even with Santa standing there, stopped, he would be crushed!

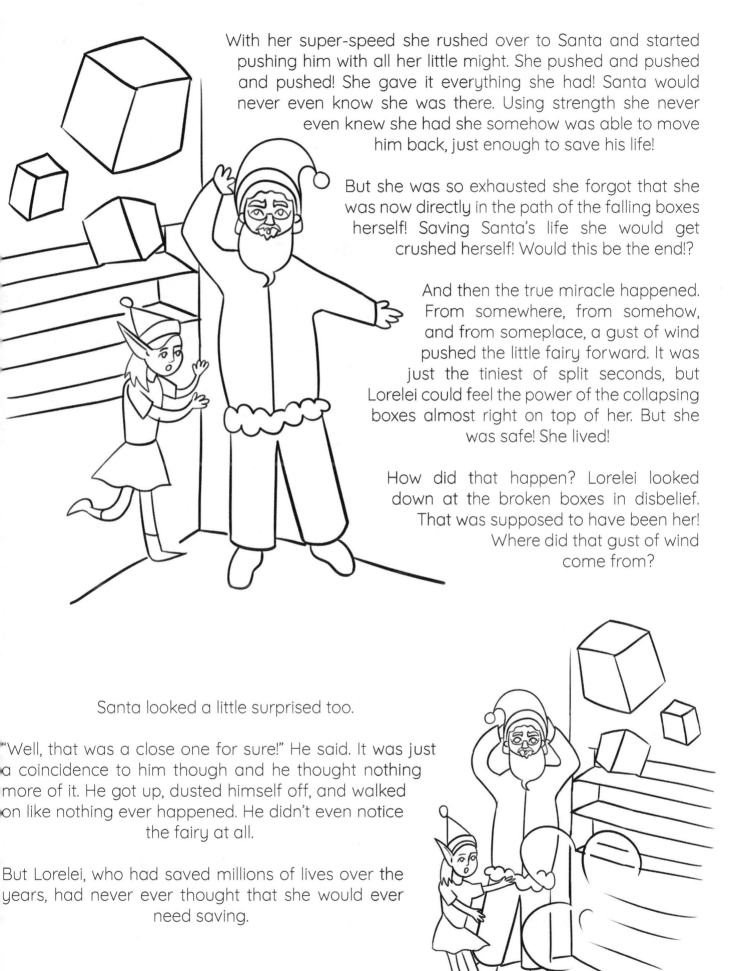

With her super-speed she rushed over to Santa and started pushing him with all her little might. She pushed and pushed and pushed! She gave it everything she had! Santa would never even know she was there. Using strength she never even knew she had she somehow was able to move him back, just enough to save his life!

But she was so exhausted she forgot that she was now directly in the path of the falling boxes herself! Saving Santa's life she would get crushed herself! Would this be the end!?

And then the true miracle happened. From somewhere, from somehow, and from someplace, a gust of wind pushed the little fairy forward. It was just the tiniest of split seconds, but Lorelei could feel the power of the collapsing boxes almost right on top of her. But she was safe! She lived!

How did that happen? Lorelei looked down at the broken boxes in disbelief. That was supposed to have been her! Where did that gust of wind come from?

Santa looked a little surprised too.

"Well, that was a close one for sure!" He said. It was just a coincidence to him though and he thought nothing more of it. He got up, dusted himself off, and walked on like nothing ever happened. He didn't even notice the fairy at all.

But Lorelei, who had saved millions of lives over the years, had never ever thought that she would ever need saving.

But there is something you may never have thought of. If the fairies are so busy protecting us they too have to be very careful. For fairy bodies are very tiny and very frail, and they could get harmed very easily. But who protects the fairies?

And this was a mystery that would live on for many many many years. It was a day Lorele would never forget. Somewhere, somehow and someplace, maybe there was someone looking out for her too.

Do older Folks Also Get Presents?

You know as you get older your wishes and desires change. Did you know that? Yes, as a child you may be interested in getting a toy train set. As a senior citizen, which means someone sixty years or older, you may want to own stock, or money put into a transportation company that runs real trains, and lots of them.

As a child you may want to have a toy umbrella to go with your outdoor doll playset, as a senior citizen, you may want a new umbrella along with entirely new patio furniture for the pool area of the house, or even a whole new and improved pool, or even a new house for that matter! Wow, that's pretty big!

As a child, you may want to have a toy tractor. But as a senior citizen, twenty new actual giant tractors for the farm might just be mildly interesting.

But the question remains, does Santa actually ever grant these kinds of wishes? Or is Christmas only for children and young people?

Well, the funny thing is, as some children may not know, when people get older, they sometimes completely even forget to write Christmas lists to Santa in the North Pole. That's right. They may give to others and have learned the true value of giving as Christ had taught so long ago and they are completely happy only giving to others, but not receiving.
But what happens when someone's needs change as he gets older and no longer needs toys, but needs things like good health, nutritious food, enough people to talk to that are trustworthy friends, or having safe and enjoyable vacations traveling the world. Should they only still focus on giving or should they only focus on receiving, if they have given so much already in their lives?

George was a senior citizen. He was happy and had the same desires and wants anyone would want later in their life. Video games were too fast for him and computers were too complicated, they were always doing something wrong anyways, those machines, he wouldn't even know what a lot of those games were called. No, when it came to games, he quite enjoyed a good game of shuffleboard, which most children probably don't know, or a good fun hand of Poker, in which he would beat most kids.

Christmas was coming up soon however and there was one thing in particular that he really wanted. He didn't write a letter to Santa, though. He didn't feel he needed to. Maybe Santa was magical and just knew what he might want anyways. No, you see, George was a very hard-working man and over his younger years, he developed a few successful businesses. He worked in building things with wood, this is called a carpenter. He had a lot of people to help and gave many people jobs. He helped a lot of customers improve the look or size of their homes because over the years he really learned what he was doing and was very dedicated. Many people, he gave work, many customers, he gave a beautiful living space and so because he lived, many people were all the better for it.

He also in his spare time helped to educate children in some of the dangers of life so they would have all the information they needed to succeed in life. He did this without any pay or exchange other than seeing the improved conditions in his home towns and areas that he influenced. He really loved giving.

Because he was successful in business and had helped so many people, George, interestingly enough, got enough exchange back in terms of money, that he could actually buy just about anything he ever wanted. So, you see, asking for material things for Christmas, was not too exciting to him. He could just go out and buy them himself if he wanted to. He knew how to shop online, and he lived in a nice home and a nice car and wouldn't want anything more really.

He would never tell you he was anything special, he was just another guy who had spent his life working and also enjoyed volunteering so that children could make the right decisions in life.

He was just a normal guy, right? Not if you ask Santa because he knew that it was people like George who made the world a good and fun and enjoyable place to live. It was the common worker who did a job at his craft, who was friendly, who cared about others and set a good example, and who gave others jobs, that was really the most important person in the whole world! And a lot of the time, they are somewhat quiet or soft-spoken so they don't stand out much.

But to Santa, it was quite different. Santa had excellent values, he knew and understood these things. And he knew about people like George, he knew all about them. Furthermore, he also knew George didn't send him a Christmas list again this year. This he knew very well.

But what would someone like George want? George had everything he ever wanted in the material world. Did he need more friends or relatives to spend his time with? Well no actually, George was funny and got along with everyone he met. He easily made friends because he really cared about others. He had many many friends and Santa knew this too. But there was something that George wanted, something that he could not really buy so easily, something beyond friendship, what was this thing?

When people no longer write Christmas lists, Santa sometimes has to use his magic to find what someone really needs and wants for Christmas, because sometimes the person himself doesn't even know!

But George knew what he wanted. George wanted only one thing really, George just wanted to be in good health and comfortable with his body. Quite a different desire from that of a child usually. So different it might even be hard to imagine for a child, but that is actually what he wanted. Santa knew this.

But how do you buy health? How do you deliver health in a present at Christmas? Not so easy. George was not particularly unhealthy, he just wanted to be able to enjoy what physical activities he did, he wanted to be able to go for walks and enjoy the sunset and he liked to travel without any problems. Santa knew this. But he had to think about how best to give George, one of the most important contributors in the world, what he wanted most. He thought about it and he thought some more about it... there must be some way!

Christmas came and with it, George experienced his joy of the holiday again through giving, but sometimes it's healthy to receive a little too, thought Santa. So for Christmas, George received a letter from Santa.

It was not an object of value, or jewelry, or something beautiful. Santa only gave him a note.

George read it to himself. In it, George found a lot of information on little things he could do to keep himself healthy all the time, and things he shouldn't do. They were simple, get enough sleep, eat natural and healthy foods, take proper vitamins, and do some light exercise like walking regularly. Also included were some links on other friendly people, who were just like George, from all around the world who also had created businesses designed to keep people healthy and happy with their bodies. Some had created healthy shakes, others had made simple exercise programs for senior citizens, there were even excellent vitamins he could take so he could enjoy life.

George loved them and decided to find the right ones for him and had very little trouble with his body for the rest of his life because enough people were caring enough to care about him and teach him how to take care of himself the right way. There were enough Georges out there to lend a helping hand to him just like he had done for others.

How many Georges are out there in the world? Will you be a George when you grow up?

Fuzzy Bear's Christmas

Y ou know, toymakers don't really realize this, but it can get awful cramped in one of these boxes, thought Fuzzy, the Teddy Bear. He shifted around in his box when no one was looking.

It was still months till Christmas, and here he was just waiting to be bought by some parents to give to their kids. The department store was a lonely place to be, he just hoped some child would come by to take him home. He just hoped that he would be loved too. Many children came by and pointed at him, some seemed very interested, but there just weren't any takers.

He did have a button on him where they press it and they could hear him talk to see what he had to say, it was always really exciting and it was his little moment to shine. It was his chance to say something creative or funny. It was his chance to win over a family. Just that day a child had come over and pressed his button. Fuzzy said the most interesting thing that occurred to him. He said, "Don't buy me, I'm just too lovable for you!"

The family laughed, but it ended up being true, they didn't buy him and it was very sad. But it was September and there were many more chances.

Another day a child came up to him and pressed his button. It was Fuzzy's turn to make a good impression so he said, "Hey there kiddo, buy me! Buy me now before I start crying of loneliness!"

Again the child laughed and so did the parents, but again, no sale. The funny thing was it was true. The only thing Fuzzy really wanted was really just a little friend to play with. He didn't need to take a lot of time with anyone, if he had just a few moments with a new friend, that would be enough, for he really really loved kids.

The next day a child came over and pressed him, "Hahahahah! That tickles!"
The child laughed and called his mom over. Maybe this would be the one! But no, they ended up getting a drone and some soldier toys. Oh well, maybe he could come up with something more creative next time.

Just a few hours later he got another chance when someone pressed his button, "Knock knock, who's there? Bye. Bye who? Buy me before someone else does!" That didn't get much of a response. Man finding a family was HARD!

The months rolled on and Fuzzy realized that if no one came to pick him up soon, then he might be replaced by other newer toys. It was very possible he would be thrown in the back room with the dust and other garbage. That would be terrible! He better come up with something soon, it was December now and he didn't have much time left.

Maybe the children of today were just more into electronics or advanced toys to enjoy having a teddy bear as their best friend. Maybe they could just make friends online now and having a stuffed animal wasn't important to them anymore. Fuzzy didn't know. But he could talk, he could say funny and interesting things, why didn't anyone want him!?

Time after time, kids wanted to go to the video game section, or pick up some slime, or get some combat action figures, or dolls. Didn't they know that Teddy Bears were the most squeezable and lovable toys in the world?

And time after time, someone seeing him in his box, pressed his button to hear what he had to say. And time after time he came up with what he thought were the most entertaining and fun things he could think of, that would win over a new family.

"Hey kiddo, thanks for pressing my button, now is my chance to say words. Words!"
or
"Hey cutie, would you like to be my new Besty?"
or
"I'm a much better toy than those soldier toys, they can't even talk."

-24-

or

"Why don't you take me home? If you do I promise not to help you with your homework since I don't know how."

or

"Thanks for pressing my button, I would sing, but then I wouldn't want to break any glass."

Each time he would get a chuckle or at least a smile and it was really the highlight of his day when he got a chance to talk. But now it was only a week to Christmas and he thought he overheard one of the clerks saying that they would need to clear out the shelves after Christmas to make room for the newer toys. This might be his last chance!

There were a lot more families in the toy section these days. But the day was coming to an end and the sun was setting when he noticed a cute little girl enter who was about three years old. She was holding the hand of her mother when his eyes met hers.

She lit up and pointed at Fuzzy and had her mom take her over to him. She was just about the cutest thing he ever saw and he knew he would LOVE to be a part of their family. This was going to be his one chance! But what was he going to say? He had no idea. Time was running out. He could see the mother's finger reach towards him and then press down his button. His whole life may depend on what he said next...

But he was out of ideas! They were waiting on him now to talk now. He didn't have any more jokes in him. He only had how he truly felt. He was only able to say the last thing that came to his mind.

"Hi there you guys, my name is Fuzzy and it's really a great pleasure to meet you. When I saw your little girl walk in with you I was in love with her the moment I saw her. The truth is, I have been here on this shelf for five months without finding a home, and all I have ever really wanted in life is to have a sweet beautiful child to be best friends with and to hug my days away. If I don't find a home in the next week I will probably go to storage forever and get thrown away. If you find it in your hearts to make me a part of your family, I promise I will do my best to bring all the joy I can to your little girl. It would really make my Christmas, and from the look in her eyes, I think it may just make hers too. Won't you take me home with you?"

He looked up with pleading eyes. The little girl was almost in tears. She looked up at her mom, but she didn't need to say anything. Although her mom was puzzled actually that the little bear had so much to say, she was expecting just one sentence. But she was truly touched by the words of Fuzzy the Teddy Bear. How could she not be?

"Plus, I'm really good at hugs," said Fuzzy.

She smiled and reached over and to pick him up off the shelf and put him into the shopping cart. The little girl was so happy she had tears of joy. Fuzzy was so incredibly happy he could barely contain himself. He had never felt so much joy in his whole life!

"CAN I HOLD HIM, MOMMY?!
PLEEEEEEEZ!"

Her mother looked down at her, "Oh honey, let's wait until Christmas OK? It's only a few days away now."

"Okay, mommy." She said while fighting away her tears of happiness. She couldn't wait for that day! She couldn't wait to hold her new friend! It was going to be the best Christmas anyone had ever had! It was going to the best day of her life.

Merry Christmas.

A Miser's Christmas

When Christmas time comes around it is usually a good idea to be careful with your money, you never know if there is something extra you might need at the last minute. Maybe you had an idea for a personalized gift for someone that is a friend of yours, or for that relative that you like. Maybe you need some extra money for Christmas lights or for the Christmas dinner. There is nothing wrong with being careful with your money. Nope, nothing at all.

Unless your name is Harold Pennypincher Senior. You see spending or saving money can go one of two directions. You can help Santa out by buying gifts for anyone and everyone around you because you love them to the point where you have spent all your money and have nothing left for essential things like food and rent. Or you can keep all your money carefully in the bank and not spend any of it, even when you have a need for essential things like food and rent. If you obsessively save the money you have to the extreme, even though you need it, well then you might be known as a 'miser.'

Harold Pennypincher Sr was a miser. If he had the option to save an extra twenty cents on a slightly smaller food option he would do it. If he could save five cents on the electricity bill by keeping the lights off at night. He would do it. He did everything he possibly could to save money, including skipping lunches. Harold was a rather skinny fellow, you know. And if he ever passed a beggar on the street there was no way he was getting any of his money, NO-SIR-EEE!

Harold lived alone, his obsession over saving money fell a little into the anti-social side, you see, he was a bit unpleasant to be around, because money was far more important than people, or helping others or sometimes even keeping agreements. And so it was for his entire life, Harold had no real friends. He enjoyed the company of the birds that would visit him in his backyard garden, but he wasn't spending a cent on a bird feeder or bird food, Nope! Not a cent. If they wanted to come by, by themselves, well then that would be fine, but they would have to find their own food. He was also older now and more cautious about life than ever. If anyone ever came to the front door, well that just meant they wanted something from him. They just wanted his money so he shooed them away as fast as they could with his cane.

Harold did not have any bills. His small modest home had been paid off long ago, his electricity bill was covered by the solar panels he had put up on his roof which he had borrowed from someone else and never given back, his water bill was covered because he could just get water from the well when he needed it. Covering money for food was easy, he was unemployed and had food stamps, so he could get his groceries that way. He didn't need a car, his old rusty bicycle could take him anywhere in town that he needed. And as far as having insurance, HAH! If he was going to save money for an emergency, he would put it into his own savings account, he was responsible with his money, oh yes, very very responsible.

Over his sixty-five years of life, Harold had actually saved up quite a bit of money. Yes, quite a bit of money indeed. Harold knew exactly how much he had at every moment, but it was a point of survival for him to never EVER tell anyone just how much he was really worth, you see because then they may want some of it, No! No one would ever know. But he currently had two million, three hundred and sixty-five thousand dollars and twenty-two cents. He could probably buy a really nice home with that, or a new car, or dress himself up to help him find that special someone to share his life with, but those were all expenses, and Harold HATED expenses. No, he would take that money to the grave with him. He also didn't keep that money in the bank, they charged interest, and what a waste that would be. So he carefully kept all his money in cash under the floorboards in the top attic of his home. Anyone trying to steal his fortune would trip his alarms and would have to get past him and his very creaky stairs first, however. He protected that stash with his life. He had invested in a shotgun long ago, an effective one.

But there was one bill that always came up every year and it really annoyed Harold. And that bill was Christmas. Christmas was not a time to celebrate, or to spend time with family, no, it was just another expense. Christmas was a bill.

However, he had many things figured out already, his tree was a discarded wire tree that he had found in the trash many years ago, it was rather small. The decorations were other little trinkets people had thrown away that Harold had shined up again and placed in and around his home. As far as Christmas lights? Harold had learned how to make his own candles.

But as Harold saw it, Christmas was always an opportunity. You see Santa was an amazing person, and he could sometimes fulfill someone's wishes on that one special day. So he was careful to make sure his chimney was open and that his home was decorated so that Santa knew he had to make a stop at this house. And Harold was always careful to write Santa a letter each year asking for one thing, the one thing in life he wanted more than anything else. Can you guess what that one thing might be? That's right, Harold just wanted more money.

His letters were usually quite simple, "Dear Santa, this Christmas I would like a check for $5,000, please. Thank you."

Of course, Santa never really came through for him. But it was always worth a try. When Santa didn't give him a check for Christmas, he would try a slightly lower amount the next year, maybe that would be more reasonable and Santa would come through. Harold figured he just needed to be good. And he was good. This year, before shooing off the door to door salesman with his cane, and scaring him half to death, he even managed to greet him with a 'hello' before he did that.

AND when he yelled and screamed at the kids to get off his lawn and frightened them half to death, he even ended his tirade with a 'PLEASE!' You see, he really was caring. And somewhere there had to be a middle ground between where he was good enough and Santa would be willing to give him a check.

Each year he became slightly more friendly in the chance that he might win Santa over. This year he even said to someone who came to his door "...AND DON'T EVER LET ME SEE YOUR UGLY FACE AROUND HERE AGAIN OR I WILL USE MY SHOTGUN ON YOU AND EVERYONE YOU KNOW! Please and thank you."

AND his demands had gone down all the way to JUST $2,200. "Dear Santa, this Christmas I would like a check for ONLY $2,200. Thank you."

And THIS had to be the year. He had said so many pleases and so many thank yous it was practically spinning him in his head. If he was any nicer, he felt he might just explode.

It was getting exciting, Christmas was tomorrow. He knew he was going to get something from Santa this time. He knew it! He waited patiently by the fire, with logs he had found abandoned by the lumberjack yard. He would need his rest and hobbled his way off to bed. He dreamed of money bags and gold coins under his Christmas tree and with a tiny smile upon his face.

The very next morning, Harold got up out of bed and raced down to the tree to see what Santa had left him! Yes! He did it! Santa had left him a present! And it was FREE! Perfect! It HAD to be money, it just HAD to be! It looked like a paper small enough to be a check.

With his greedy fingers, he tore the wrapping paper to see what it was.

Hmmm...

Santa's present was a note. It said, " Thank you so much for being kinder this year Harold. I really appreciate it and I really appreciate you. There is someone that I would like you to meet. Please be at the Tea Palace tomorrow at noon." Included was a gift card for the Tea Palace, so the meeting would be free.

Well, that was not very exciting, definitely not the few thousand dollars that he wanted. Just a $20 gift card! Hmpf! Santa just must not really like him.

But it was free so the next day he made his way to the Tea Palace. He sat by the chair in the corner which had his name on it. There was also an open seat. He enjoyed some teas, it was some of the finest he had ever had, he LOVED the taste of free! It was delicious. Then a stranger made his way to the table and sat down. He was also an older man just like Harold and looked him over.

"Now just who the hell are you!?" he said.

"Well, I'm Harold Pennypincher. Now who the hell are you!?" he replied.

"My name is Scrooger McDaniel! And I got invited here by Santa... wait your name is Pennypincher? Are you a miser by any chance?

"ME!? A miser!? No, I'm just very careful with my money, why are you a miser?" Said Harold.

"ME! No no no, I just know how to save money."

"Oh? ...and just how do you save your money?"

Scrooger answered and they got into a rather long conversation on how to keep from spending money. All the different strategies and methods of how money could stay in their pockets, and not go into anyone else's pocket. They talked for hours and hours, it was a fascinating conversation for both of them.

Soon they realized that if they lived together, they could cut their property tax bill IN HALF! And they could share small expenses. And did you know that if they got just a few bigger and better solar panels, the power company could be paying THEM for their electricity!?

But most importantly, for the firsts time in his life, Harold had someone he could really talk to, a friend he could share his life with, and someone he could really save money with, a fellow miser. They would live out the rest of their lives saving thousands and thousands of dollars more together, than if they lived apart. It was glorious, it was the best present Harold had ever gotten. Santa was a genius!

A very Special wish

A special alert had come into the North Pole in early December that year. The Special Wishes section had received a very special request from a young boy. This was a very different section than other sections because you see, you had to meet two very special qualifications for a Christmas wish list to end up in the special wishes section.

You had to one, be extraordinarily, supremely and enormously and incredibly good! That was the first qualification. And secondly, you had to put in a request that while practically almost impossible, was at least remotely, in some way shape, or form, humanly and physically possible. It wasn't completely impossible, it was just 'almost' impossible.

Santa only got about ten a year and this day was one of those days. He gathered all the elves around him and opened the letter and after he had everyone's attention he read the letter aloud, it was from a young boy by the name of Quentin who was eight years old.

Santa cleared his throat, "Dear Santa, You are the bestest bestest bestest man in the whole world, each year you give me the best gifts ever and Christmas just makes me happier than anything. I have been looking forward to Christmas ALL year and it is finally almost here. This year I would like just one thing, Santa can you give me my very own space ship? You see I need to explore the moon a little. I will continue being the best boy in the world. Thank you so much."

Santa looked at the group of gathered elves.

"Now, what could a boy of eight possibly have done to deserve a spaceship!? I mean even adults don't have spaceships! They are dangerous, the technology of space travel barely exists on Earth. People have died trying to make their way to the moon or come close to dying. We would probably be hurting him more than helping him if we grant his wish. When was the last time anyone ever even went to the moon? Show me his qualifications!"

The elves had documents with him giving the history of Quentin's life's accomplishments. In bold capital letters, the beginning of the document made it very clear that he was a boy of only EIGHT years of age.

Santa read it very carefully... then he read it again.

"Oh!" he said.

Then he read some more.

"Oh! Aha!" he said.

Then he read it again to the end.

"Mmhmmm. Mmmmhmmm. OK, I see." he said, "Well..."

Apparently, the boy was quite intelligent. He had learned to read at the age of two and by six he was already studying advanced calculus as well as advanced physics and rocketry. He was even responsible for inventing a more efficient flying technology for personal and commercial drones. He even created some toys for kids to order online which enhance the stability of drones in flight. It was because of the boy, that thousands of children the world over had kept from flying their drones into trees due to the safety features this boy had invented.

"But wouldn't he be rich already? Maybe he could buy his own spaceship!? He probably doesn't need me!" said Santa to the elves.

"Yes Papa Santa, but there is only one real problem with that." said Grimey, one of the elves, "Children eight years of age don't really manage their own money and also, you see, spaceships kind of don't exist on this planet. People haven't been working on it very much. So you can't really order one. They have to be built!"

"Well!" said Santa, "We are not engineers. I mean we can build some amazing things definitely and we even have advanced toy sections with all the latest electronics and video games and consoles. But for us to build an actual working spaceship, well that's practically almost impossible!"

"ALMOST, impossible. Almost" said Grimey.

Santa thought it over, "Well, the boy is super smart, but is he also kind?"

"Oh yes sir, the kindest!", said Grimey

"All right, well is he caring, does he help others when they ask for help?" asked Santa.

"Oh always, he actually goes out of his way to help others even when they don't ask for help Santa," said Grimy.

"OK, ok, but is he polite, does he say words like please and thank you?"

"Oh always Santa, always!"

"Hmmm, ok then." He thought it over some more and after discussing it some more he got up out of his large red chair and made his way over to the phone...

* * *

Christmas time came and Quentin couldn't have been more excited! He had been SOOOOO good that year, he knew he had to get that spaceship. Oh gosh! Exploring the moon would be the funnest thing ever! Maybe Santa would even make it submersible and he could take it underwater too. Wow! He was bursting with joy. He ran down the stairs to see what presents were there for him on Christmas morning.

Disappointingly, however, there was nothing there large enough to be a spaceship. There was nothing there that was big at all! Every gift was actually quite small. Hmmmm, had Santa forgotten about him? That didn't really make sense.

He looked through the gifts and some were for his sister and some for his brother and then he found it. "To Quentin, From Santa"

Oh boy oh boy oh boy. He opened it. What!?

It was a diploma. A DIPLOMA!? Quentin didn't want a diploma, but why?

There was a note by Santa on the diploma, Quentin read what it said.

"My dearest Quentin. You are a very very special boy and your contribution to mankind will never be forgotten. This is a very very rare occurrence but I regret to inform you that for once, I actually cannot grant you your wish. I cannot give you the spaceship that you wanted.

The only reason I can't give it to you is quite simply and easily because I don't know how to build you one that is safe enough and fast enough. But there is someone that can. And my boy, that someone is you! It is upon shoulders like yours that the future of man rests when it comes to reaching for the stars as only a small handful of people would ever be smart enough or willing enough to even try. You are really the future of mankind.

Enclosed you will find a diploma. I spoke to your school and you are way ahead of everyone else including even your teachers. You are now graduated from High School and University and you are needed in one of the few companies in the world that is actually working on the problem of getting man into space. Here is your pass to work there for free on an Internship, you will meet their Chief Executive Officer in Orlando, Florida, and together with him and their other brilliant minds you will learn to build a real spaceship not only yourself but for all of the rest of us to follow. I'm afraid you are far more qualified than me!

You are super super special and it is only through children like you that our future depends. I will always be watching you from above and good luck with the rest of your very special life. Much much love, Santa."

Quentin was floored, he never felt more validated in his life. His whole life took a shift at that point, he no longer needed to go to school! It was a little boring for him anyways, but he had so many friends there, he would miss them but always remain in contact with them.

He made a lot of new friends in Orlando however, and for the rest of his life he dedicated himself and all his talents to the betterment of mankind and it was through his efforts that man was more easily able to reach the moon and then Mars and then Alpha Centauri and finally the stars themselves.

The Dragons Mystery Present

In all the lands, across all oceans, and through all skies,
There exists one creature beyond all norm and earthly ties,
A creature so powerful and strong that it owns one and owns all,
A creature that only needs to stand to make the world appear small,

For that creature is the mighty Dragon of Legend,

But even the mighty female Dragon had a problem weighing heavy its head,
As it watched with loving eyes her baby dragon cub toss and turn within its bed,
Snow had begun falling outside the windowpane,
Replacing all thoughts of warmth, of sun and of rain,
Winter was upon them,
And that could only mean Christmas time would be theirs again,

What to do, what to do?
For the child that had all a mother could ever give,
A child that had all the colors of the rainbow from green to red to brilliant blue,
That had all the toys ever made through and through,
That had all the kingdoms men at beck and call,
That had all the pets in the world, even a kangaroo,

She went searching her cave for the perfect present,

She looked for ideas, for inspiration,

What she found were mounds of golden treasure and all the wonders of civilization,
She found artwork, and crafts and charming little trinkets,
The walls adorned with Christmas decoration,
But to give she found nothing,

They were peaceful dragons,

All their riches and spoils were friendly offerings of the people from the towns
All the friendship and gifts arriving from daybreak to sundown,
For the dragons were loving and happy to protect,
And the common folk, their adoring subjects,
Everyone loved them, from beggar to highest Crown,

Perhaps she could enlist their help,

There must be something that would that her child would love,
Perhaps a cardinal, or a blue jay, or a dove,
But pets they already had aplenty,
There was simply nothing she could think of,
All she really had to give was her undying love,

But there had to be something,

She knew she had to make it a very special day,
Christmas Eve was only a few days away,
It was the most precious of times and everyone's favorite holiday,
A day filled with joy and cheer and play,
But not without fresh new presents,
Her hands empty, and her heart filled with dismay,

But then a thought occurred to her, an idea sprung forth,

A plan set in motion, an idea was born,
There would be something to fill that very special Christmas morn,
She knew exactly what to give that with which her cub could play and play,
Everyone rushed to work, make way,
Ready the banners, sounds the horns,
Preparations were to be made for the coming day,

The moments passed and not before long,
The townsfolk had gathered in one great big throng,
For it was Christmas morning and our little Dragon cub,
Was slowly awoken by the singing children's song,
Come one and come all, they sang, come along,
For our prince and future dragon would soon be awake,
And open his gift, a gift to be treasured for a thousand years long,

He rubbed his eyes and made his way to the tree,

Under the tree there was but one present, just one,
What could it be, a jewel? Gold coin? A water gun?
Normally a bounteous array of presents filled out the tree,
But this time it was just one,
As the cave began to be lit by the slowly dawning sun,
Wrapped it was in finery and had to be undone,

With an eager heart, the dragon cub unwrapped her one and only present to reveal,

An egg,
It was an egg,
It was quite a large egg,
It was not an ordinary egg,
"What is it mother?" asked the cub,

"Well, my young beauty, you know us dragons we live for thousands of years,
And the coming of a new dragon cub is a time for great joy and cheers,
It is a very very rare time indeed for one to be born anew,
But for Christmas this year your father and I thought we would give to you,
You're very own sibling to share your life with"

The cub stared down in wonder at the egg,

It was at that moment that there was the slightest tremble and a quiver,
A small tiny crack, and a stir,
And an even small-clawed finger,
revealing a new life,

It was a day no one would forget for many ages,

Merry Christmas

The Falling Cat of Christmas

Falling falling falling went the cat,
Falling went the cat of Christmas,
Falling falling falling went the cat,
and with none to bear witness,

Just why he was falling he did not know,
Nor did he know where he came from, or where he would go,
Looking up and down there was little to see,
A very strange situation I'm sure you'll agree,

Worried he was, for what would he land on, and would he survive?
From such a great height, and such a swift falling dive,
Through clouds and mist, he continued,
Perhaps he would fall forever he mused,

It was dark and he couldn't see his friends,
He tried to find just where the world started and where it ends,
But he made little progress, even through the glasses lens,
But just then he saw a tiny spark of light,
Something was blocking out the darkness,
Something was parting its way through the night,
What could it be? Was it a fairy? Was it a sprite?

He waved his hands and shouted out "Hello!",
He shouted and shouted at the only warmth in the night, the only glow,
It seemed to respond to him, or was it just his imagination?
It had stopped moving and seemed to approach according to his calculation,

From out of the darkness, the light changed shape, and took form,
And with bright jewels and colors, it was adorned,
"So pleased to meet you, I am Tilly"
"I am a sprite and I can fly", it was so happy to inform,

Tilly looked over the cat's situation,
Where ever was it going? Did it have a destination?
Falling falling falling went the cat,
Falling went the cat of Christmas,

"It's very nice to meet you, Tilly, I am the cat of Christmas"
"Normally I am on grounded, but something very strange has come to pass,"
"You see I lack the ability to fly,"
" But for some strange reason, I seem to be falling out of the sky,"

He looked down below in hopes that something would stop him,
Something soft, like water, so he could swim,
He looked at the flying sprite and said,
"If I keep falling, can you tell me what may lie ahead?"

The sprite took one look and replied,
" I wouldn't know for sure, but it looks like you're having quite a ride."
"But would you like for me to fly you home to your bed?",
"Otherwise you could hit something hard and hurtful instead,"

"Yes, yes that would be wonderful,"
"My bed at home is warm, and made of wool."
So the sprite used all its power and all its strength,
To break the fall of the cat it stretched out her wings to their full two inches length,

But it was to no avail,
The cat was simply too big, it was set to a much bigger scale,
And so falling falling falling went the Cat,
Falling went the cat of Christmas,

Despair filled both their hearts when suddenly to the cat it occurred,
That she was special and she could feel reassured,
That she was a cat and cat's were different,
All cat's had abilities that were truly magnificent,

For all cats had lived numbered nine,
And their feet and limbs had a special design,
That no matter the distance and no matter how hard the concrete,
A cat will always land on her feet,

He looked again, he looked below,
At what appeared soft and white, much like snow,
But it wasn't snowing at all,
What she saw were mounds and mounds of pillows,

He looked over at the sprite and she realized,
He remembered where all this had begun, he surmised,
It began when he became sleepy,
So that he had come from pillows and would go to pillows again he was not surprised,

He looked back at the sprite and waved goodbye,
As he watched his little friend return back into the sky,
He had been dreaming of Christmas morning,
And then had passed into sleep without warning,

But now it was time to wake,
To see what wonders of Christmas would be his to take,
For he was the falling Cat,
He was the falling cat of Christmas,

He opened his eyes and this time it was for real,
The falling stopped and only the soft blankets and pillows he could feel,
His sight was filled with wrapped presents,
Oh, what wonders did they conceal?,
He was so excited as he stretched and licked his heels,
He was falling no more,

He had finally landed and landed he did in the most wonderful day of the Year,

Santa had left his magic and had flown off with all his reindeer,
It was a time to smile, to feel joy, and to cheer,
And so did the Falling Cat of Christmas,
Open his presents with a great big smile, from ear to ear.

The Lazy Goose

Once upon a time, there was a lazy goose,
The days were slept away, her work schedule loose,
Of her chores, she would simply defer,
As wasting away the days she preferred,

But of her Christmas wish list, she was very careful with her time,
As leaving anything out would just be a crime,
She had many many things she needed and wanted,
And so she put her full faith in Santa undaunted,

Santa would be the one to save her lack of makeup and toys,
Santa would be the one to keep her safe from all the boys,
Santa would be the one to fill her tree,
Santa is the one, she said, you'll see!,

So she sat in her room by her clock,
Watching the time tick away, tick-tock and tick-tock,
She sat in her room all alone,
And yet all across the floors, her clothes were thrown,

There was much to do,
For hard-working Mother Goose had to keep home from becoming a zoo,
But always more things to get done would accrue,
There was so much to do, very very much to do.

Yet the lazy goose sat in her room and just watched the clock,
Idling away her time, tick-tock and tick-tock,
She said she would work, but was that just talk?
Her body in the chair, back and forth she rocked,

Then one day Christmas finally came,
Santa had been watching closely, to her shame,
While her wish list was very complete and very long,
From her actions, her needs and wants an abundance of rewards did not belong,

So what did Ole Saint Nick leave our lazy goose under the tree?
Was not what she had asked for, how could this be?
Wasn't every child in the world to be satisfied on that blessed day,
To have everything coming to them they wanted in every which way?

Instead of an abundance of presents that Christmas Eve,
Sat just one present, and instead of joy our goose had to grieve,
But what was inside, what could it be?
Santa was always so smart and kindly,

She unwrapped her present only to behold,
What looked to be a calendar of beautiful white and marigold,
But it wasn't a book or a calendar at all,
It wasn't something she could read, or hang on the wall,

It was an organizer.

Wait what!!? An organizer!!?

What does she need an organizer for? That's not a real gift,
She stormed out of the room all quick and all swift,
Her thoughts in a daze,
her mind sent adrift,
Why would Santa ruin her Christmas?
She did nothing bad, she was not on the naughty list?,

After many hours of grieving and crying,
She finally returned to see what else there was to see with her eyes drying,
Santa had left her a note,
What did it say,
The goose read the words with a heavy throat,

"My dearest friend, you are lucky today,
For while other children sulk and other children play,
You will learn the most important lesson of life,
One which will stay with you, and will not go away",

"Other children don't know,
that the best way to live life is to show,
Your love for your fellows by what you can do,
By being honest with yourself and by letting your love shine through,"

"Your actions are by what we can judge you,
You completed deeds define you,
And with a plan and a goal,
You can win too,"

"Your mother is so hardworking and she's having all the fun,
But there is so much joy to be had, honest, there is a ton,
For at the end of each task, is a reward,
and a building of trust that will and last and last,"

"And should you fulfill your work and chores,
By the coming of next years Christmas you will have all you ever wanted and more,
May your days be spent active and your muscles be sore,
And your nights be spent sleeping, resting your bones while you snore,"

"I will see you next Christmas and you will see,
Your Christmas will the best it can be"

The lazy goose looked again her organizer,

Each day had some chores, not too little nor too much,
Some days needed strong hands, others just a soft touch,
Each series of chores had an end with a reward,
And rather than aimlessness, she had something she could work toward,

The days passed and passed and her Mother was so thankful,
That she had raised a child so caring and so helpful,
More time passed and the lazy goose had finally learned,
That life was to be lived, and the rewards that she got,
Were just so so much better when they were earned,

As the months grew on that calendar year,
She knew that Santa would be along again and bring with him all his reindeer,
And this time it would not be the same as the last,
For this time she would get everything that she asked,

An even longer list for Christmas she made,
And she got every last thing and more and in spades,
She was so thankful indeed,
For Santa really knew what she did need,

It was not a new bedspread and not a new toy,
All she really needed was to learn work and in life, she could find joy,
Merry Christmas

The Aging Toymaker

There once was a toymaker who was a master at his craft,
But alas, as the years rolled on he found he was very understaffed,
For you see our master craftsman in question,
He worked alone with no one there to help him,
In his youth, he could easily fill every order,
No matter the volume, no matter the ardor,
He just worked and worked his fingers to the bone,
Making all kinds of wonders from toy cars, to dolls to toy phones,

But he was older now and to his dismay,
Sometimes he had to leave his orders to be complete the next day,
Then late one night much to his surprise,
He woke to find all the toys made and all the dresses sized,

He got up and stood from his stool by the bench,
To find nothing left out, no fabric or nail or even a wrench,
All the dolls in a row by the ferns,
All work was done, even his returns,

What could have done this, but why question why?
Time that morning was already passing him by,
He looked at his next orders and never gave it much thought,
He just went about by his business and that was a lot,

For the whole day, he worked and finished his woodwork,
He never ever took a real break, that was one of his quirks,
But before he knew it the midnight hour had struck,
And to bed, he never made it, all comfy and tucked,

The orders had been pouring in that day once more,
They got to be so much he just stuffed them in a drawer,
For he knew he couldn't keep up any longer,
His hands were wrinkled now and his bones weren't getting any stronger,

But once more that morning he rose to find,
That someone somewhere had been very very kind,
All of the orders he had stuffed in a drawer,
Had been completed and there had even been more,

For with all the work done,
His entire workshop was left clean and even the tables had a sheen,
Never before had the toymaker even thought,
To keep all his tools and projects without a spot,

He began to wonder if he fell behind again that night,
Would the same thing happen the next day with the morning light?
But it did not really matter to him,
He had things to get done and work he did through thick and thin,

The next morning he woke to find that,
Everything was once again done, he didn't even need to feed the cat,
He didn't need to shine his shoes, he didn't need to hang his hat,
Because someone else had somehow done all that,

It slowly started to become a norm,
He didn't have to complete every task, he didn't have to work up a storm,
He did what he could and he still worked very hard,
But if he couldn't get to it all his ego wouldn't be marred,

For the very next morning, everything would be done,
Everything from toy trains to dolls to toy guns,
Curious though it was,
He noticed somehow as he cut and as he glued,
That he was running strangely low on cat food,

He had an idea, one that might not go over well,
It was something he knew he may never be able to tell,
He put out some more food by the fire,
As well as a box, some string and a wire,

And the very next morning the toymaker found,
That the box trap he had laid was now making a sound,
Slowly he lifted the box to see what was inside,
To find a tiny elf now had the box occupied,

"Well, that was not a very nice thing to do,
With all the help I've been giving you,"
Said the tiny being with a high pitched squeaky voice,
"Maybe next time you can make a more friendly choice"

The toymaker stared with eyes in amazement
He had never seen anything like it, and very quickly he did repent,
"I'm so sorry my small friend for I just did not know it was you,
Who's been helping me all this time to pull through"

"Maybe instead of sneaking and secrets, I recommend,
that instead of being strangers you and I should be friends"
The elf sat back and thoughts went through his head,
He was clearly uncomfortable and so he said,

"Santa told me to come to help you here in the shop,
He told us how hard you work and that you never stop,
He said that with your toys you give joy to many,
That it was high time you had help and not just any,
"He said you deserved the best in the world,
And so he sent me, My name is Earl,"
The toymaker stood there and then said,
"Well, it's pleased to meet you, I am a toymaker, my name is Ed"

And so that day a new friendship was formed,
And two cold hearts were warmed,
For together they worked and got much more done,
And even started having some fun,

When the toymaker felt tired and had to go for a nap,
The elf would take over and fill in the gaps,
For food, the elf no longer had to forage,
Because the toymaker was more than happy to provide him with porridge,

So, on and on they worked until the rest of their days,
Fillings kids stockings and making the holidays,
They became better friends and closer and closer,
until through natural times passing they parted ways,
Better friends there never were.

Santa's Last Mile

It was Christmas Eve and Santa had delivered presents to millions of children,
For thousands of miles and across the seven oceans he had ridden,
It was now 4 in the morning and he was tired,
But it rested on Santa to deliver their wishes and to fill all their hearts desires,

Cold and dark was the winter night sky and it had started snowing,
The wish to go to sleep with warm hot chocolate inside him was growing,
Only in the North Pole,
Could he relax by the fire and hot coal,

An elf seeing Santa struggle,
Had thought the best motivation possible and close to Santa began to snuggle,
He showed him letters from the kids while through the sky they were swerving
And what they had done to be deserving,

Little Tommy had made his parents beds for a month without being asked,
Little Johnny had mowed all the lawn down to the last,
Little Jenny was on time for school the whole year,
Little Ellie made sure her home's windows were clear,

Little Ted for the fireplace had chopped wood,
And Little Andrew made breakfast for his baby brother whenever he could,
So many children and so many good deeds,
Lead Santa on through the night with newfound speed,

The more tired he got the more the Elf read,
The more Santa declared "Full speed ahead!",
And it was only due to the love and the care of the children through the cold snow,

That Santa completed the last of his journey with all reindeer in tow,
The next day he would be fast asleep and how exhausted he was none would ever know,
But Christmas was delivered and was once again was on time,
Because the world was filled with so many loving and helpful children,
Merry Christmas to all.

Zoey the Ice Cube

Zoey was an ice cube living in the Arctic. He was not just any ice cube however, Zoey was as tough as tough can be. When others asked for help, Zoey didn't. When others needed directions, Zoey already knew where to go. When others needed a shoulder to cry on, Zoey definitely had things under control. Zoey was tough as nails.

As sometimes happens, way up in the Arctic circle, where it is as cold as it gets, weather can change around quite often. Sometimes it can snow. Sometimes it can get windy. On some days, it can get very very cold indeed, especially in the wintertime. But sometimes, just sometimes, on some lucky afternoons, the Arctic circle can warm up.

As the months went on and Christmas was on the horizon, for some strange reason, by some strange twist of fate, due to some mysterious circumstance, a warm spell hit the North Pole and all our little ice cube friends with it. What would it mean? Would our little friends melt? Would they shrink in size? Only time would tell.

The warmth was something, however, that our friend Zoey didn't need. It was something he didn't want. It was something he actually didn't like. In fact, it was even a little dangerous to him. But he didn't worry, Zoey the ice cube was tough and didn't need anyone's help. Not even during the warmth that December month. He took to himself and found his own way, others would see how strong he really was, while others were complaining about the heat, he would let his worries take a back seat.

Truth be told, Zoey was so tough, he was a little feared by the other ice cubes. They didn't want to talk with Zoey. They didn't want to get yelled at by Zoey. They didn't really want to be friends with Zoey. This was because you see, Zoey was really really tough. He was also very big and tall and strong.

As the week passed, the clouds seemed to be making their own preparations for the holiday, for they were nowhere to be seen. In their place was the sun. The bright, shining, and oh so strong and powerful sun. It would shine through the morning. It shone brightly in the middle of the day. It shone through the afternoon and only when the sunset did the ice cubes come out to play.

Ice cubes knew how to have fun, skating along on the frozen water and chasing each other, playing hide and seek, and by dancing. Because of the strange weather, all of their playings had to be done at sunset, or after dark. The whole town of ice cubes had to hide in the shadows as best they could.

But not for Zoey, Zoey was too tough to be playing games. He didn't need to play games with anyone. He didn't ever lose. And he was so tough in fact, he didn't even need to hide from the sun in the shadows. No sir! Not Zoey. Zoey went out in the broad daylight and walked and walked showing just how tough he was. He walked with very strong powerful steps to show the other ice cubes just how tough he was.

But something very interesting happened. The stronger and harder he stepped. The weaker his footsteps became.

Then something else interesting happened. The deeper and harder he tried to make his voice, the lighter and softer it became.

Then something else happened. The more he tried to stand over and above his fellow ice cubes, the shorter he became.

And while he was out in the sun all alone, all the townsfolk huddled together in a group. While Zoey was out working in the sun, all the townfolk were inside working in the caves as a group. And while Zoey was out showing how tough he really was, the townsfolk were spending time together showing each other how much they loved each other.

As the weeks before Christmas passed, the townsfolk, staying closely huddled together, became stronger and bigger and made one big strong ice cube as a group. And Zoey, being all out alone in the sun shrunk and shrunk and shrunk until finally, he was all but a tiny spot.

The townsfolk were no longer scared. The townsfolk were no longer frightened. The townsfolk were no longer wishing to stay away. For the townsfolk had plenty of love to give. And so it happened that they welcomed him with open arms. Was that perhaps what real toughness was all about? To love in spite of all?

Zoey, being just a droplet had no choice but to accept. With the last of his strength he tried to make his way back to the group, but sadly he failed. He fell into the snow. Did he disappear?

The giant ice cube that was the townsfolk raced out of the cave and looked for Zoey in the snow. After many minutes of searching, they were able to finally find him, and with love, in their hearts, they hugged him and hugged him until he was a part of them. The ice cube town had rescued Zoey before he melted! Zoey was overwhelmed with his own feelings of thankfulness. He had never felt like this before. Maybe this was how life was meant to be? Played and enjoyed with others he thought? Maybe he was meant to work with others? Maybe being close to others made him stronger.

Over the next day, he grew stronger, but only if he stayed near his new friends. And it was that night that Christmas Eve came to pass and Zoey knew that through some miracle, through some magic, through some change of fate, he had received the best gift of all. He learned the precious gift of love.

Merry Christmas.

The Lonely Spinning Top

Many toys had come through Santa's workshop over the years. Many Christmases and many millions of kids meant many millions of toys were created right here in the workshop in the North Pole by Santa's elves.

From year to year children's favorites changed and changed. One year everyone wanted trading cards. That fell out to be replaced by fidget spinners. That then fell out of favor to be replaced by surprise hatching toys. But when that got boring it was replaced by electronics.

In fact, Santa had to add an entirely new building in his workshop just to be able to produce electronic toys. One part of this new workshop was dedicated to video games. Another part of it was dedicated to tablets. Yet another part of it was dedicated to making computers even!

Children's wish lists were getting more and more technological. Santa was not someone who would be left behind the times, and as long as kids were doing their chores and working hard where they were supposed to, he made sure to keep up with the latest and greatest toys no matter the times.

But with so many newer toys being asked for, sometimes older toys had to be put aside. And so Santa had a building put aside where all the unused toys would go and be stored. It was a lonely and sad area of Santa's workshop in the North Pole called "Storage"

No toy ever wanted to be put into storage and left. They all wanted children to play with them. Sometimes, however, they got lucky and with time passing, people realized how valuable and precious these early toys really could be, and they really went up in value and everyone wanted them again.

So it was with many many toys. They even became collectible in some cases, no matter how simple they were. All toys seemed to go through that cycle. All toys you see except one. All toys except Whizzey, the spinning top.

What is a spinning top you ask? Well, you see that is something a child from the '60s could tell you with ease. But a child of today may never know that a spinning top can be one of the funnest toys ever, Just ask Whizzey! A top is a circular toy meant to spin round and round on a tiny point. You just have to give a spin and see how long you can keep it from falling. Could you keep it for a minute?

But Whizzey wouldn't know you see. He was in a corner in the dark hidden under some cobwebs. Once every few weeks it got really exciting because one of the elves would open up the door, shed some light into the room, and at least let little Whizzey see what's around him. If he was really lucky maybe some child wanted him and he could have a new playmate! That would be the most exciting thing of all. Or maybe he had even become a collectible.

But no. Time and time again, the elves had come in for some other toys. One time it was so exciting, the elf even had to shift little Whizzey over to the side to get to the toy he needed. He didn't come for him, but it was still so very very exciting.

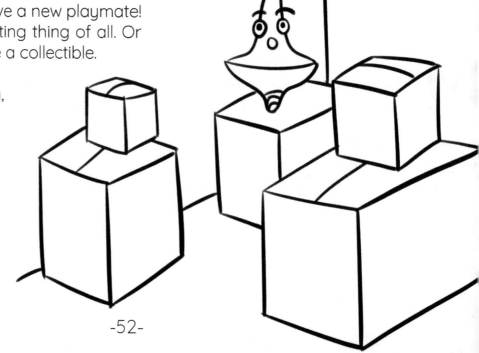

It was nearing Christmas time and something very very exciting happened. There had been a renewed interest in older toys and collectibles and the Storage room was being scoured for toys people would want. They were doing a cleanout.

They were getting closer and closer. Soon they would have to pick him up, they would have to! Closer and closer and then... it was over. They left Whizzey in the corner where he had always been. Did they not see him?

Whizzey felt very sad. He felt left out again as he had for the last forty years. I guess kids just didn't care anymore about tops. Other toys had replaced him. He felt a tear roll down his face. He couldn't help himself, and he burst into tears.

Crying he continued for what seemed like forever. Then there was a sound, someone was at the door and entered. He seemed to be looking for something. Whizzey stopped crying for the moment. He looked over in wonder. The elf had come near him! Was it his time finally?

He shuffled and then turned around again... and Whizzey burst into tears once again. Just at the moment, the shuffling feet stopped...
"What was that?"
The elf turned and looked around. It was coming from the corner. He walked over and our little friend bawling his eyes out that he had been one of the last toys left alone.
"And just who might you be?"

Whizzey stopped crying and looked up in disbelief that someone was actually talking to him.
"Well.."

He could barely talk.

"My name... my name is Whizzey"
"Whizzey eh?" The elf reached down and picked him up. True joy was bubbling inside Whizzey just at the feeling of someone holding him for the first time in many many years.
"And just what do you do? You look very simple."
Whizzey couldn't believe the excitement he started feeling. Could someone actually be interested enough to give him spin again?

The elf was fascinated. He put little Whizzey down on the floor and give him a mighty spin! Wshhhhhhhhhh went Whizzey! He was never more alive and never more happy than at that moment. He just kept spinning and spinning and spinning! It was like he would never fall down again! He just kept spinning and spinning!

The elf looking on was waiting for him to fall, but he just kept on going, it was amazing to him. After several minutes, he picked little Whizzey up off the ground and held him high again. "Well, you certainly are something special! I think I'm going to show you to the rest of the elves and keep you as my own."

And so it was. Whizzey had a new playmate, but it was never what he expected at all. He lived out the rest of his life in the North Pole as a toy for the elves to play with. They tried to see who could spin him the longest and Whizzey loved every minute of it. Even though he was dizzy as can be he never felt happier. He had everything he ever wanted and the elves even modeled other newer toys after him. It was like he had his own children that went into new homes. He was alive again, he was happy again and he was playing again. And Life was good. Merry Christmas.

The Princess who Didn't Believe in Santa

There once was a Princess who lived in a magical land. It truly was a magical land. It had fairies, it had unicorns and it had elves. Princess Lucilia even had seen them with her own eyes, flying between the clouds, she had even talked to a unicorn! But there was just one special someone that she never saw. And that someone was none other than Santa Claus himself!

She didn't believe in Santa in fact. She never saw him actually. It must be someone else that left her the gifts under the tree each year. It was probably just her staff who did it. But now she was old enough, she knew she could prove it. Christmas Eve was that night and there would be no doubt! She would show the world that Santa was just an idea, not a real person. It would be undeniable. It would be certain and it would be for sure.

Her plan would pan out flawlessly, the steps would roll out perfectly and her strategy would work out beautifully. She knew exactly where to sit on her steps over top of the fireplace. No one would see her. She knew exactly where to put the camera, no one would ever suspect it. And the final piece of her master plan, well it was just too brilliant for even words. In fact, it was so smart, she hadn't told anyone. No one would know her secret. And when she had won and proven herself right, she would announce it to the whole world, THERE WAS NO SANTA!

She was almost more excited about her being right about this than even the gifts she would receive. Every year, with her being a princess, after all, she would receive a mountain of gifts. It was almost too many some years she had to admit. And she was always very careful about writing her Christmas list months in advance so that nothing would be left out on that magical morning. But you see THIS year would be different. This year would be very very different! For this year, she purposely left out the single most important gift of all. The one thing she truly always wanted but never had. She left it out of her list, but if there was a Santa, a real Santa, then he would know what she really wanted and he would bring it to her, without her having to write it down. If she didn't get it, and if Santa never came down the chimney, then she would have final proof!

For the gift that she had always always wanted was a deep secret tucked away in the back of her mind. Something that only she would ever know. The thing she always wanted was a unicorn of her very own. But unicorns were so magical and precious and so rare, that even a princess and the highest of royalty could never truly own one. Unicorns were left to their own cloud kingdom far above the humans and were left to roam of their own free will. But nevertheless, that is what she always wanted, and she had been a very good girl all year long. Santa would either know this and appear and bring her gift or he would not. Christmas Eve was just about starting and only one of two things would happen and Princess Lucilia was very excited! She would either have her very own unicorn, or Santa wouldn't exist.

The secret camera had already been placed between two flowers near the c e i l i n g where no could ever see them. She had taken many naps during the day so she wouldn't fall asleep that night, she would see if anyone actually ever came down that chimney. I mean come on, how could anyone fit through that chimney at all, much less a fat person. It was completely impossible! AND she had all her snacks at the ready so she wouldn't get hungry. She tucked herself into the spiral staircase above the hearth of the chimney right where she could have a perfect view. She had already fooled her helpers into believing she was in bed. And her little hiding spot was even in the dark. It was perfect! Even she marveled at her own planning.

Now it was just a waiting game. She suspected that Old Saint Nick would typically come in, in the middle of the night, probably at 4 in the morning when everyone was fast asleep. No problem, she would stay awake all night if she had to. But she knew no one would come, so it would be kinda boring. Which is why she brought herself a book.

It was now midnight, she was holding strong, she knew Santa wouldn't be coming along. The clock passed 1 am, she was enjoying reading her book with her tiny candle. Then 2 am in the morning passed, still nothing. It was no surprise to her, she didn't expect much. Finally, 3 am struck and her story was becoming ever more interesting. But she had to admit, she was getting sleepy. She tried to keep her eyes open as best she could. There was only one chance in the year where she could prove the truth. She tried her best to stay awake, but wait! Was she imagining those elves, were they just part of her storybook, or were they real?

She ate some more chocolate! That would keep her awake. Yes, that was elves in her story. OK, she put the book down and focused on the chimney. Nothing would stop her. Her seating position was a little uncomfortable, nothing like her bed, but she could do it. She had slept all day. But, somehow the fireplace seemed to be getting dim, however. She couldn't explain it, and then suddenly it happened. She fell asleep! The truth would have to rest in the camera she placed and what would transpire in the morning.

It was Christmas morning when our princess woke to some screaming and shouting!

"Alas Alas, the princess is gone! She has disappeared! Where is she?!"

was being shouted both near and far.

They didn't know Lucilia was quietly tucked away here in the banister by the fireplace.

She decided she had better show herself. Getting up she found she was quite sore, not sleeping in her bed was not something she had done before, and she had fallen asleep. She made a quick survey of the presents under the tree, nothing was there that resembled a unicorn, that was for sure. Quickly she ran over to her camera to make sure it had recorded and IT DID It had worked, she just needed to fast forward to 4 o clock to see what happened! Or to see, rather, what didn't happen. But she had not the time, quickly she ran over to her helpers and to her family and enjoyed another beautiful Christmas. This would have to wait.

She opened present after present and got everything she had desired. Diamond earrings! A jeweled tiara! The fanciest dresses money could buy! The list went on and on, but, no unicorn She knew it!

Once all the presents had been given and all the meals had been had and all the performers had finished for the evening, she raced to her room as fast as she could to watch the camera footage and tomorrow she would make her announcement!

She fast-forwarded the video, there it was! 4 AM, PLAY! She watched as nothing happened just as she thought. She could even see herself falling asleep in the corner of the video. Since there was nothing happening she fast-forwarded it some more. Again nothing much occurred, but then... there was some sort of motion or disturbance. She went back and replayed that section to see what happened because the camera was tilted to the side after that point.

There was a shaking like the night watchman was making his rounds and somehow upset the camera. She watched it intently! There were some sounds happening, but she couldn't be sure where they were coming from. Then a bump! And... the camera, while still recording, but was now only recording the side of a wall!

"Well, that does me no good!" she said.

She couldn't prove anything with that tape. It could have been anything that caused that bump. The nightwatchman was always making his rounds around the house. But surely it couldn't have been...

"Oh what a waste!" she said. But she still had proof, she had been really good all year and still didn't get the unicorn. But she was tired. Tired from having slept on the stairs all night and she plopped her head down on her bed when she noticed something strange. Her head fell against a hump under the sheets! She moved the sheets aside to see what it was.

Well! It was a unicorn! But it was only a unicorn plush toy. It wasn't a real unicorn, this didn't prove anything! But wait there was a note there as well. Hmmm... she opened it and read it.

It wasn't a note at all. It was a map! Well, that was odd. The map leads to a giant tree and some clouds. Princess Lucilia was fascinated and raced out of the house, and with some guards to help her, she followed the map. She ran across the fields. She swam across the brook and she climbed the giant tree.

Then she found, there was a path in the clouds leading up. But surely, you couldn't walk on the clouds, could you? She took a careful step and WOW! She could walk on this cloud! She took another step... and another. Up and up it took her like a staircase. The guards looked on in wonder. She made her way up into the clouds. And then she found it!

What she saw was like heaven if there ever was a heaven. Rainbows stretching across the clouds every which way. Clouds for trees and... unicorns! Many many unicorns! Just then a smaller very beautiful unicorn came and approached Lucilia and nuzzled up against her face. They were instant friends! The princess gave her a giant hug, the biggest hug anyone had ever given anyone before. It was all her dreams come true! She looked again at the map, and she noticed there were some strange initials in the corner... S.N.

The Dinosaur with an Attitude

All the kids in the Dinosaur neighborhood knew Christmas was on the way. They were on their best behavior at all times, for they knew that Santa would be watching. The better they were, the more gifts they would get. That was for sure. Some even went out of their way to do good deeds, even when no one had asked anything of them.

All the kids were doing this. Well, all the kids, except one. Sammy was not really an ordinary kid, you see he lived in a valley of the Raptors. There are many many different species of dinosaur. Many are actually quite peaceful and live on a diet of plants, like the Brontosaurus. Some live on a diet of meat, but even they can be friendly, especially around Christmas. But the Raptor, well, let's just say he is a fast and aggressive species who doesn't like to mess around.

Sammy, while the other kids were busy building caves and huts, felt that they would be the perfect testing grounds for his jaws, so he tore them down. And Sammy, while the other kids were busy, playing with each other and having fun, was hunting any and every animal he could. Sammy, while the other dinosaurs were singing Christmas songs, was busy practicing his fearsome roar to scare people off. But what set him apart was that he was at least TRYING to be a better dinosaur, he didn't want harm to come to those around him, he just couldn't help himself.

Santa knew this was the case when he called to have a special meeting among his elves. He had warned them that only the bravest of elves should attend this next meeting. Because this mission would be one of the most dangerous of all. An elf was about one one-hundredth the size of a dinosaur, and really they were the perfect sized food for a dinosaur. But most of all when learning about Sammy, he learned was not the friendliest of dinos.

Santa assembled the group of twenty of the bravest elves and once he finished explaining the situation, and that the mission was in Dino land, 18 of them immediately drew back and weren't interested. He only had two volunteers left. But when one of the volunteers found out that Santa had said "dinosaur" and not "Convenience Store" he immediately withdrew and didn't want to volunteer anymore.

Which left only one brave little elf. It left little Tommy. The bravest elf in all the North Pole.

"Well, I daresay Tommy, you are the bravest elf in all of the North Pole!" said Santa.

Tommy, stood proud and said, " Don't you worry Santa, I'll take care of Sammy, by the time I'm done with him he'll be the most well-behaved Raptor you've ever seen! And the elves will have a wonderful time making all sorts of presents for him for Christmas time."

And so Tommy shipped off on his own sleigh and made his way to Dino land and the valley of the Raptors. It was a little scary trying to hide from the giant flying Pterodactyls, but Tommy made due. He made his way to the village and called out for Sammy.

"Hey, has anyone seen Sammy!?", said Tommy.

"Last we saw him he was tearing up the cottage over by the river," said one, pointing up the road.
T
ommy set foot on the path hoping to find his Raptor friend. All the while pretending to be calm and not scared to death talking to dinosaurs that towered above him.

He walked and walked and then heard some commotion up ahead which he thought could only be Sammy.

"HALT RIGHT THERE!" yelled tiny little Tommy to the much bigger Dino.
"Do you know what you're doing there?"

Sammy looked around but didn't know where the sound was coming from until he looked down. Oh! There was a tiny little elf. Sammy sized him up, almost as if he was food.

"Don't you even think about it, mister! You eat me and you'll never get another Christmas present again in your life!" yelled the little elf in his high pitched voice.

Sammy backed off, "Wait, did Santa send you? I wrote him a letter about my not being able to control myself and my needing to be a dinosaur. Did he send you?"

"You better believe it. And starting off by eating your own elf helper is not going to help you any! Now, do you mind explaining to me what you're doing there with that cottage?" He motioned to the cabin that was in the middle of being chewed up by the Raptor.

"Oh that!? Well, I was just testing my jaws to make sure that they were strong enough. Well, no problem thought the elf. We are going to replace cabins with tree trunks. Using his small body he pushed him over to a small group of trees and let him chew up those instead. Little Sammy the Raptor felt better already.

"Now, what other problems are you running into?"

"Oh well, I have a tendency to eat anything and everything that comes near me that is smaller than me."

Well no problem, thought the elf. "Have you eaten me? He asked.

"No, come to think of it, I didn't eat you!" He started feeling even better.

"Perfect, in fact, you are actually in charge of protecting me FROM being eaten and you are doing a great job of it already. Now, do you like seeing people smile?" He asked

"I LOVE seeing people smile!" said the Raptor.

"Perfect, now you're going to find the nearest creature and without crushing it you're going to give it a huge hug. Now go!"

So Sammy went out, and with his great speed, ran around until he found a rabbit, and then carefully, gave it a big hug. Then he put the rabbit down and watched it carefully. The rabbit not used to such friendliness couldn't help but smile and this made Sammy feel EVEN better.

"Wow! This is really working" he said.

"All right, from now, you give hugs, no eating every single living thing. OK, What else are you having trouble with? Asked the elf.

"Well, I kinda can't keep myself from taking things that don't belong to me." Said big Sammy.

Well no problem, thought the elf. " I see. Well, do you have any possessions that you really treasure?"

"Hmmm..." The Raptor thought it over, "I have a teddy bear that I really love."

"Perfect! Now imagine how you would feel if someone took that from you."

The Raptor looked sad.

"Right, now imagine if you had lost your Teddy Bear and someone returned it to you, how would you feel?"

The Raptor brightened right up.

"Now you are going to return everything you have taken that didn't belong to you and you are going to apologize."

The Raptor went around town and returned everything and saw how happy that made everyone and felt EVEN better!

"Well geez!", said Sammy, "If I can make other people feel happier then I feel happier"

"That's right my friend. Now we only have three weeks left before Christmas. You are going to go around and rebuild everything you have destroyed and watch the smiles you are putting on the other dinosaurs' faces when you are done."

Sammy did just as he was asked and was very careful to protect his little new friend the Elf. No one could go near him! When Christmas finally rolled around, Tommy took all his belongings and made his way to the North Pole, Sammy found he was twice as happier than he was before waved goodbye. The elf reported to Santa what had happened, and with a town that was back to normal and one really really happy Raptor with two new Teddy Bears for Christmas, everyone was as happy as can be. All it took was a little brave elf with a little understanding and a lot of care to make things right. Little Tommy, the elf, was a legend from that day on.

Santa's Sleigh Needs a Little Help

Santa was getting ready for the big night. Christmas Eve was only 3 nights away and millions and millions of kids were ready for the big night. For the North Pole, that meant preparation and more preparation. Everything had to be perfect. The candy canes had to be numbered out, the Reindeer needed to be trained and rested. The toys needed to be all made and tested and most importantly of all, Santa's sleigh needed to be in perfect condition.

The elves were working away like mad. With Christmas so close, it was not a time to relax for anyone, there was an excitement in the air and all-around Christmas music was playing while everyone sweated away. Unlike a lot of other machinery, however, a lot of Santa's tools of the trade ran on magic and on the belief of children in the miracle of Christmas. Because it is the belief and love of the children that brings Christmas to life each year.

Everything was checking out just fine, the toys were being inventoried and were all in a row, Santa's bag was magically endless and would hold all the toys, the reindeer were ready, Santa's belly was empty enough to be filled with thousands of cookies and milk, but there was one problem, however. The sleigh was not meeting its recommended numbers for safe flying. It wasn't quite flying fast enough, it wasn't flying quite high enough and it wasn't flying quite steady enough.

This had many of the elves quite worried and they hadn't told Santa yet, but they somehow had to fix the problem, and they had to fix the problem in the next two days. Santa had enough on his mind already anyways, not to be worried about something like this. They would need to figure it out. They had tried to adjust the skis, they had fed the reindeer the finest herbs and grass they could find, they had tried to make the sleigh with a lighter material. But nothing worked, with thousands of miles needing to be flown, the sleigh would not make it all the way.

They were starting to get desperate. Tobi, the lead design elf pointed out that they would need to somehow need to increase the belief and love of Christmas for children around the world to set the sleigh to rights. But how would they ever do that in two days?

Another day ran away from them without any solutions.

"Maybe children just weren't as excited about Christmas anymore!" said one elf.

"Maybe the children didn't have as much of a love of Christmas anymore!" said another.

"Maybe children just don't believe in Christmas anymore like they used to." said yet another.

Still no answer, but the hour was getting late and it was time for Santa to make his final preparations. He boarded the sleigh and all the reindeer were in position. Because of the clock, Greenwich, England was the first area of the planet to have Santa visit in the very early morning.

And before anyone knew, Santa boarded the sleigh with his bag of toys and they were off! The elves on the ground carefully eyed each other with very worried looks. Tobi was very nervous.

Santa began the routine of delivering the presents one home after another and made his way through Europe. But it wasn't before long that he noticed the sleigh was sagging a little bit.

He arrived at the next home and plopped the sleigh down on the roof to get out. The reindeer stood by obediently and hung on. Santa went down the chimney and began delivering presents when it happened! The sleigh started to roll off the roof! He heard a weird sound and then heard a bump. There was a lot of blackness outside on the lawn! Santa ran over to the window to see what had happened. The sleigh had fallen off the roof and onto the front lawn!

He ran out and checked on the reindeer, they were a little surprised but they all seemed fine. Wow, the sleigh never seemed to have many problems like this before? Could the children of the world not have as much belief in Christmas as they had in other years? Would he be able to finish delivering Christmas to everyone around the world?

Just then, little Chrissy, who was an eleven-year-old girl living in the home was rocked awake by the sound of the bump. She heard some sounds and ran downstairs to see what had happened. She didn't believe it would be Santa, it must be an intruder and she had her phone ready to call for help. Quietly and in the dark she crept forward and looked out the window.

She couldn't believe her eyes. She saw Santa and the reindeer on her front lawn! Wow! Christmas was real and here was Santa right there! But what was he doing on the lawn? And then she only had one thought, this was the best opportunity for posting an update to her phone of all time!

She snuck around the side, where she knew the floodlights were, and got her phone ready to capture a video. Santa seemed to be looking after things out there as something might have gone wrong, so she had time. Then she did it! She turned on the light and pressed record.

"Ho ho ho! What's happening here!? I can't see!" Santa put his hand to his face to cover some of the light and stepped back. After a few moments, he noticed the little girl.
"Ho ho ho, there you are Chrissy! And what are you doing up at this time of night? Shouldn't you be safe in bed?"

Chrissy was shocked! "I just heard the commotion and I went down to see what was going on. Wait, how do you know my name?!" said Chrissy, then she looked around.

"Oh, ho ho ho! Surely you know who I am don't you? Well, I just ran into some trouble with the sleigh. I'm not sure I can finish Christmas, I am running behind already."

"Oh, that's terrible! What do you think is wrong?" asked Chrissy

"Well, you know kids have not been believing in Christmas as much as previous years. And this sleigh runs on the hopes and dreams of all the children in the world together. It looks like I may not be able to get her off the ground again. But nevertheless, I have something for you. Here you go"

Santa handed Chrissy a small present, wrapped in purple with bright ribbons. Chrissy was amazed. Christmas really was amazing!
"Is this what I think it is?"

"Oh, ho ho ho! Well, you know what you asked for?" He gave a wink.

Chrissy knew what she wanted, a personalized necklace. It was a light box, just the right size and weight for what she asked for. She looked up at Santa. She was SO excited!

"Oh!" said Chrissy. Then she had a bright idea! She stopped the video and posted it! She titled it, "Santa gets stranded on my front lawn and Christmas is canceled"

First, she posted it for her close friends. It was in the middle of the night, but some of her friends were awake on the other side of the planet. The video looked so real, because it was, and so interesting, also because it was, that those friends sent it to their friends. Then those friends sent it to their friends. And then it happened, the video went viral and before anyone knew it. Santa's troubles were being viewed by millions of people and all around the world all in the space of about forty-five minutes!

It occurred then that the sleigh started moving a little on its own and started glowing. When Chrissy showed Santa all the children's well wishes and hoping he would be able to fix the sleigh and more and more kids started to believe, it seemed to make the sleigh come alive. Carefully, Santa stepped in and tested the controls.

Yep! Everything was set. The sleigh was just suddenly working again! With a great big smile and a thank you, Santa waved to Chrissy as he took to the air. He was in a hurry now to catch up on his schedule. But Chrissy had saved Christmas! What a miracle. Chrissy went back to bed, but that morning when she went to open the present Santa had left her, she found that it was the necklace that she asked for but that it also had a special inscription, Chrissy, the Savior of Christmas!

The Dancing ornaments of Christmas

It was Christmas Time and night had come to replace the day,
Unbeknownst to many, it was time for Christmas ornaments to
come out and play, Waiting patiently during sunlight,
With winks and silent tells, they waited for the night,

Waiting they did for the adults and children to retire to bed,
Occupying the home they did with their dance in the humans 'stead,
What adventures they had would always be left unsaid,
Dancing in circles under ribbons and lights of green and red,

Played they did while the humans in their beds turned,
Lit by the soft light of the fireplace last embers burned,
How much went on the humans never really learned,
And only when the creeping morning sun came, to the tree they returned,

This is the story of two ornaments, the princess and the elf,
The elf was the full embodiment of elegance itself,
Matched only by the beauty of the princess quite the elegant queen herself,
Together they danced every night from the living room floor, up to the highest shelf,

Each night they would secretly eye each other waiting for the right time,
For the grandfather clock to hit the last of the days chime,
For them to leave the tree,
For them to feel alive, for them to dance and for them to feel free,

But with secrecy being of the utmost importance,
They had to be careful not be revealed by sound, and to leave their night lives to chance,
For together they only wanted to just love each other and to dance,
They could lose it all with a simple humans glance,

And so they danced and they danced,
But they danced in silence,
Careful not to wake anyone, or to touch any presents,
They danced and they danced, their joy of life and of Christmas immense,

What song they danced to was anyone's guess,
The elf holding the princess in the sweetest caress,
The princess always tumbling and whirling in her finest pink dress,
No one, their love they could suppress,

Sad it was that while they danced they had nothing to dance to,
Waltzes, ballroom dances, ballet, each night something new,
They knew all the moves and holds tried and true,
The more fun they had, the more their love grew,

Then Christmas arrived and with it, many presents were revealed,
Happiness and joy Christmas presents unsealed,
And many glances the elf and princess would steal,
Senses of longing and desire would be healed,

There was something for everyone to enjoy,
There were clothes, there were books and there were toys,
There was something for the girls and there was something for the boys,
But there was also something that was making a strange noise,

However noise it was not when it was completely wound up,
It was a gift that seemed to be for no one, a gift that didn't seem to add up,
When a child read the card it only read,
That it was meant for a certain charming fellow and a certain red-head,

Dismissing the gift as some kind of mistake,
The humans took back to their laughter and to their cake,
And to the more presents, Santa had left them to take,
But the elf and the princess looked at each other at each free moment, at each break,

For the gift was not just another set of clothes or some socks,
Someone had gifted to the family a music box,
For it did not seem accidental,
That the only music it played was soft and gentle,

The music box on the shelf the family left,
And the elf and princess in this Christmas day were blessed,
For very carefully during the nightfall,
Their day would begin with a celebratory ball,

But only a few days remained now that Christmas had passed,
And making the most of their time together, they made memories to last,
For every night just once,
They played the music boxes song until silence once again would come,

They would hold each other dear,
Because being close to New Years it was their fear,
They would soon be put away, and would see each other only next year,
But together in a box, they would be near,

And so it came to pass that with music in their hearts they said goodbye,
And despite the long time, their love would never die,
Merry Christmas,
We will see each other again and with dance may our love again magnify

Christmas in Africa

With Christmas comes many wonderful wonderful things. Things like presents, things like candy canes, and things like trees, But there was one thing Little Kwame wanted to see more than anything else that he had never seen before. He wanted to see snow.

You see in Africa, it was warm and while it snowed in many other parts of the world, Africa never had any snow. It was this thought that struck Santa when he was reading Johnny's Christmas list.

"Surely there must be something else the boy would like." He said, scratching his head.
There was only one thing the boy wanted. The boy wanted to see snow on Christmas.
He looked over at some of the gathering elves.
"Has this boy been good?" he asked.
The elves looked at each other and shrugged.
"Yes sir, he's been the best-behaved child in his entire village in fact."

"Oh boy! I can make many things happen, but I'm not sure I can make it snow in a hot climate..."
He looked around.
"Do we still have those fake snowmakers?"
Then he looked back down at the list and noticed the word 'real'. The boy only wanted to see real snow.

"Ok well, where is this village located? Is it somewhere up North where it may snow nearby?"
The elves got together and pulled out a map.
"I'm sorry sir, the boy lives in a town called Habari. It's as hot as it gets over there. The nearest snowfall would be a thousand miles away."

"Oh boy!" said Santa. He thought about it but then was interrupted with another pressing matter and left this problem to another day. Would he be able to create a miracle?

Maybe if he became a famous soccer player, he could travel the world and go to places that had snowfall? But it was said that Santa could grant any wish. So for the whole year, Kwame, before going out with his friends to play, made sure to complete all his chores. Before going to school, he made sure to make his bed and pack his lunch. The dishes were always done because of Kwame, and all year long before his mother even asked anything of him, Kwame had already done it.

But what she didn't know was that Kwame was only doing it to be a good boy, what he really wanted for Santa to watch him and grant him his wish. All year long he thought about it. Every day he thought about it. Almost every hour he dreamed about it. Was it true? Well, he looked again at the calendar and the clock, it was only 4 more days, 13 hours, 29 minutes, and 12 seconds before he would find out. He was bursting with excitement!

Habari was a poor town and last year, the only thing Kwame got was a small carved zebra, which he kept by his window. He loved his zebra, but he wasn't the best-behaved boy that year but this year he was a five-star perfect boy for sure. Santa would take notice, he knew it.

Time passed and the magical night finally came. Kwame got up out of his bed, along with his brothers and sisters to find... his mother had cooked a very nice breakfast meal for all of them, eggs and stew and for Christmas, they would have... a very nice dinner made with the finest meats and vegetables from the larger town. They did not have a tree, they did not have presents and they did not have decorations. They were a poor family, to have a wonderful Christmas dinner was still very exciting. Kwame was not disappointed with that. He knew that day was not over yet, and having a great dinner with everyone would make wonderful memories.

The day passed and they had their feast and it was time for Kwame to start putting things away. Again, he did so without being asked. He was happy to do it. Then he made his way to his room. But on his bed, he found someone had left a note. He opened.

It was a ticket. Hmm. A ticket meant that he was allowed to go somewhere. Maybe it was somewhere special. Maybe it was somewhere that had SNOW! Curious though, because it didn't say where to display the ticket. Who did he give it to?! He looked around and there was no one. It was starting to get dark and soon he would have to go to bed. Maybe this was somehow connected to his Christmas miracle. Oh well, he started getting ready for bed and put everything away.

He had a bit of a restless sleep when he heard a knocking on his window. It wasn't a person, it was some kind of animal. Commonplace in Habari.

"Shoo! Shoo! I'm trying to sleep" Kwame said as he turned his head. But the noise continued, even while he tried to hide under the covers. It just wouldn't let up. Kwame was just about to yell something else when he noticed a light coming from outside.

He got up out of bed and walked over to see what was going on. The light was coming from one of the reindeers. Wait what!? There were reindeers! There were no reindeers in Habari! He went outside and found a sled, that was connected to reindeers. They all turned and faced little Kwame as if expecting something, one of them muzzling him. He began to pet them but they somehow didn't seem satisfied and they kept muzzling him. Then he had an idea!

He raced back inside and grabbed it. It was the ticket. He was going to give it to the reindeer, but like magic, it glowed and then seemed to evaporate into the air and disappear! But the door to the sled opened up!

He got on board. It was a little scary, as it was still very early morning and there was very little light. But he trusted the reindeer. He got on board and fastened the seat belts it had hung on. Seconds later they were in the air whooshing away to somewhere new.

He saw his village under the cover of darkness but couldn't see very well. He was scared he wouldn't be able to see anything from the flying sled. He looked to the horizon and realized it was very early morning. The sun was very slowly creeping out of the mountains. Wait the mountains! Of course, Kwame's father had always told him about the great Atlas mountains of Africa. The top of the mountains would have snow! He was so high in the sky, he could feel it start to get cold, but he didn't need a jacket, he loved the new experience! Then he felt what seemed like a soft rain hitting him, but it was somehow weird. It came in the form of little flakes with fancy patterns... SNOW! Wow!

He opened his mouth to try to get as much of it as he could to take with him, but it all seemed to melt away as soon as he saw it. Then he flew over the top of the mountain and could really see the beginning of the sunrise. The whole mountainside was covered in snow. It was amazing, it seemed to take on the color of the sunrise in a brilliant pink and purple. Kwame would never forget this moment as long as he lived. He enjoyed the moment. Then as fast as it had come, the reindeer flew him back, his parents might worry. But it was ok, this was the best day of his life and he would never forget it. Just as he was getting out of the sled the reindeer motioned toward the compartment by the side of the sled, there was something there.

It was a brand new shiny soccer ball! Santa had got him a brand new soccer ball! Kwame was overjoyed and couldn't stop smiling. This was the best Christmas he ever had! It was the best DAY he ever had! He vowed to always be good for the rest of his life.
Merry Christmas.

The Boy who would Inherit Christmas

"How many years had Santa been flying his sleigh and delivering presents?" Thought little Asher. How many years has it been? Thankfully, Asher had his tablet now and could look up any question. Let's see what google thought...

He typed in 'Santa Claus' in the search. Hmmm, that didn't really answer much. He tried to do a search for 'Christmas' Hmmm... also not many answers other than there are presents and trees.. let's see, he added the word 'history'.

OK, here we go! So Santa has been delivering Christmas for two millennia... OK, that's good but what's a mil-le-nia? OK, he looked it up in a dictionary. Wow, so it's a thousand years! He has been creating Christmas for two thousand years! That's amazing! But how could anyone live that long? He must be very old. Very very old. And very magical. Very very magical.

He thought it over when just then he got an alert from a friend sending him a message. He ignored it as he had more important matters to sort out, like how did Christmas really work anyway? He swiped it away.

He had another thought. If Santa had only one night to deliver these presents, and there were so many families on Earth, then he would have to deliver them to all the families of the earth. And that was a lot of families, and I mean A LOT of families. "Hmm, I wonder how many families there are on Earth?", thought Asher.

"That's what google was made for", he decided. He typed his question and got some interesting results. So, there were currently about 7.8 Billion people on earth. Wait, what does 'bil-lion' mean? OK time for the dictionary again. It means a thousand million, ok. But what's a mil-lion? OK, dictionary. OK, so that's a lot of zeros. Hmm... how many families is that? OK so... yeah. A lot!
Santa must be very fast. Very very fast. And very magical. Very very magical.

Which left him with one final question, how does the sleigh fly? I mean is it gas-powered? Is it just magic? He typed it into google. Ok, so it seems It flew because Santa passes electricity through the runners on the sleigh so the superconductors can… wait what's a superconductor OK, the dictionary says it's a material that can transport electricity. Well, it sounds fancy. Santa must be very smart. Very very smart. And very magical. Very very magical.

Just then, Asher got another message on his tablet. He swiped it away. This was too interesting. He wondered if he could somehow help Santa, I mean if he is so busy and all his main work falls upon one single day of the year. He wondered how he could get a hold of Santa to talk to him and ask him some questions. He looked online to see if there was any way to contact him somehow. Let's google search for how to contact Santa. Hmmm…

Just then a friend messaged him. "WHAT IS IT! I'M BUSY!"
He looked at who was messaging him. Oh, wait it was someone he didn't know. How did someone he didn't know message him? Hmmm… Oh well, this person went by the name of Klaus. And he was asking for me to look by the window.

But wait what? Klaus? Was he German? Hmm, seems familiar. He was on the second floor so looking out the window probably couldn't hurt. He peered out and… there was an elf sitting on the window sill!

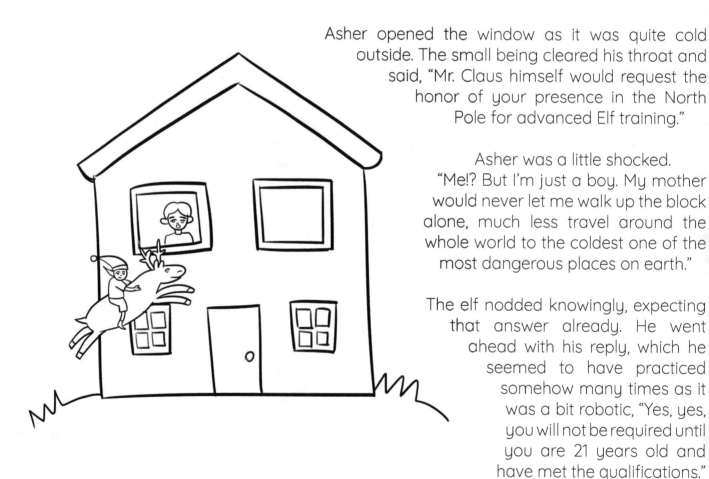

Asher opened the window as it was quite cold outside. The small being cleared his throat and said, "Mr. Claus himself would request the honor of your presence in the North Pole for advanced Elf training."

Asher was a little shocked.
"Me!? But I'm just a boy. My mother would never let me walk up the block alone, much less travel around the whole world to the coldest one of the most dangerous places on earth."

The elf nodded knowingly, expecting that answer already. He went ahead with his reply, which he seemed to have practiced somehow many times as it was a bit robotic, "Yes, yes, you will not be required until you are 21 years old and have met the qualifications."

"Qualifications? And why does he want to meet me?"

The elf continued, "you will be required to meet these requirements. 1. You must be a Grade A good boy on Santa's Nice List for the next 11 years in a row. 2. You must study the following volumes, 'Magical Transportation and Sleigh Maintenance' by A. Frost and 'Endless Toy Bags and their Properties' by J. Mistletoe and pass a test and finally 3. You must demonstrate your willingness to help Santa by organizing going door to door singing Christmas Carols to spread cheer for the next 11 years. If you meet these requirements then on your 21st Birthday you may travel to the North Pole to meet with Santa."

Asher took it all in. So Santa must have some help. Learning about magical transportation? Reading couldn't be more interesting actually! Singing Christmas carols? He loved to do that anyways. And being a good boy? Well, that was the easiest thing ever. Hmmm.

"And can you tell me why he wants to meet me then?" Asher asked.

"Santa is getting on in years you see, and should anything happen to go wrong he needs a backup plan in case anything ever happens. He needs a team that's ready to go at a moment's notice. But they need to be trained in incredible speed, incredible strength, be able to withstand super cold conditions, be able to fly in almost complete blackness, be organized enough to be able to deliver the correct presents to 2.2 billion homes in 24 hours across the world without error. This is no easy task. Every year Santa chooses the brightest and most helpful children to be his back up and only very few are ever chosen. He wanted me to visit you to offer you your chance.", and with that, the elf gave a salute, put his letter back into lapel and jumped down off the roof into the bushes, and ran into the darkness.

Wow! Thought Asher. It was true, he was getting the best grades in his school, and he was on the Honor Roll, and he loved helping others. Maybe doing the right thing and being a friend to others had its rewards after all.

It was Christmas when he received two extra gifts. It was the books the elf had talked about. Amazingly, if anyone else looked at them but him, they appeared to nothing but empty notepads with nothing in it. But when Asher looked upon the two great big books, he saw complicated and advanced instruction on magic and flight. It would take him years to fully understand what was written within. He made a vow to study them as hard as he could, to always be as good as he could, and to have some fun getting some friends together to do some caroling. After all, Santa couldn't do it all himself could he? If Asher was ever needed, he would be ready!

Reindeer Racing

Santa's reindeer numbered twelve in total,
Their ability to travel the skies was global,
Many days and nights they spent waiting for that one day,
So with their extra time they talked and they played,

Many games they had to idle away their time,
Playing together was their favorite activity, it made them feel sublime,
From Antler Ring Tossing to Tag to Hide and Seek,
They would spend their time playing week after week,

But as time passed and Christmas came near,
Only one game it was that to them was most dear,
Because while regular reindeer the world over are in amply supply,
There are only a few handful magical enough to fly,

And fly they did from sea to shining sea,
With brilliant speed, they traveled over every town and every tree,
They traveled the world and under the cover of night,
Their spirits lifted right up whenever they took flight,

But their spirits never lifted higher than when chasing,
And trying to come first in reindeer racing,
It was the funnest way to put to the test,
Just which of the reindeer's speed was the best,
They raced across the toy factories and across fields of white,
Their heights soaring high and theirs turns tight,
They went across towers and cathedrals and all manner of things,
And they did so without any wings,

Their racing field was many many miles across,
Turn right the orchard, fly over the school and left at the Churches cross,
All twelve of them raced,
And once in the air all fears and earthly concerns were erased,

But every year one the biggest of the reindeer would normally win,
He would be past the orchard while the others would just begin,
He flew so fast he was practically a blur,
He blasted by the trees and gave them a stir,

But this year a new reindeer had come to the race,
Who had strong aspirations of first place,
She knew she could fly fast and outpace,
And have even the fastest of reindeers have her chase,

Her name was a little different, it was Everlast,
But don't let her name fool you, she was faster than fast,
It was the last race before Christmas and everyone knew,
Whoever won now, would be whom everyone would look up to,

She took to the starting with her magical speed in tow,
And when the starter pistol went off she put on a show,
She went so fast you couldn't tell her blur from the snow,
Feeling her fly past was like being in a tornado,

She flew past the orchard and flew past the school,
Only to find her rival next to her, it was a duel,
For miles, they were neck and neck,
They were so far ahead, to the others they were just a speck,

But then the final turn came around,
Passing the cross they flew to the finish line, both victory bound,
Who would win it was so so close,
The remaining reindeer just watching now, had froze,

For the last few meters, it was at last determined,
They crossed at the same time, it was confirmed,
They were both a winner and so Santa had said,
Let them both this year lead the front of my sled,

Another year has gone and the reindeer knew,
It was now time to fly for the Children and that they did do,
Merry Christmas to One and Merry Christmas to All,
The Reindeer were now ready to Answer Santa's Call,

The Melting Snowman of Summer

Christmas was a time for a lot of fun new things, decorations, candy canes, ornaments, and more. Little Benny absolutely loved everything about Christmas right down to his Chocolate Christmas calendar. But there was something that Benny looked forward to more than anything else, even more than the presents. Little Benny loved building snowmen.

He would make them as big as possible. Twice as big as himself, sometimes even three times as big. When he put on the carrot nose and the button eyes they were in the beginnings of coming to life, but once the scarf and the jacket and the hat made their way onto the snowballs, for Benny, they finally became real.

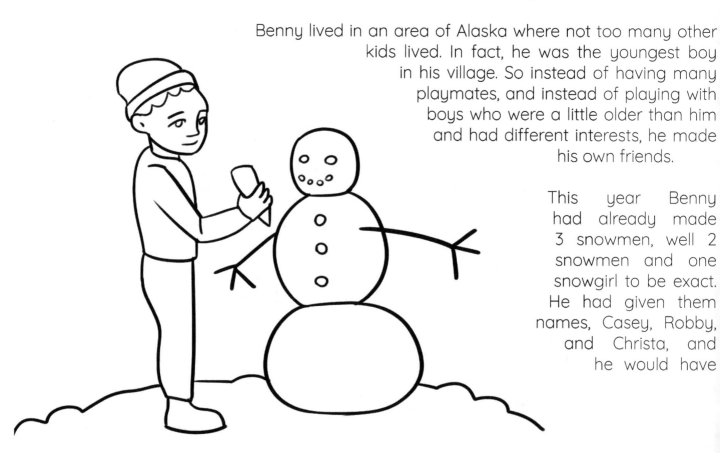

Benny lived in an area of Alaska where not too many other kids lived. In fact, he was the youngest boy in his village. So instead of having many playmates, and instead of playing with boys who were a little older than him and had different interests, he made his own friends.

This year Benny had already made 3 snowmen, well 2 snowmen and one snowgirl to be exact. He had given them names, Casey, Robby, and Christa, and he would have conversations with them. He was always very careful to only go outside to build them once he had finished with all of his chores. And he was also very careful to use clothes and buttons and carrots that wouldn't be used by his family anymore. No, they went to a much higher purpose. It was like he was building a second family.

The village town of Kiknuk was very high up on the Equator and it really made for some of the best snow. The finest snow to build with was always the softer kind, Benny waited for a day for it to harden just a little, and then he got to work. Today he decided to build his next snowman, but this time his new family needed a boy, so this one wouldn't be so big.

"What shall we call him Christa?" said Benny.
Of course in real life, Christa the Showgirl didn't reply. But that didn't matter because in Benny's imagination they always responded.
"Hmmm how about Willy, I've always liked that name." She said

"WILLY! Willy, it is."

Benny got hard to work on the base snowball, rolling it around and around, anticipating the moment that he would be able to speak to it and befriend it. He had everything he would need, he had all the buttons he needed from the tailor, he had the carrot that he needed from his mother, he had the jacket he would use from the used clothing store throwaways.

He spent the next hours making the other balls and with all his might he packed them on top of each other and started putting everything together. It was starting to get dark when he was about to make his way inside his house for dinner when the snowmen bid him goodnight.

Wait what? The snowmen bid him goodnight!? Well, it was just his imagination again. He really did have a powerful imagination after all. So he said, "Good night to you all too."

He made his way up the steps when there was a gust of wind and it almost seemed like one of the snowmen waved to him. He couldn't be too sure though because the sun had set and it was a bit windy. But no matter, it was dinner time.

The rest of the night went on as usual and after a wonderful meal, Benny made his way to bed and dreamed of more adventures with this snowman family.

The next day after his homeschooling with his mother, because there were not enough children in the town to make for a schoolhouse yet, Benny couldn't wait to get outside to play and work with his snow friends. But he noticed something else odd, it seemed like one of the snowmen was smiling. Well, it wasn't the snowmen, actually, it was the boy, Willy. Benny didn't remember putting a smile on him, but there it was. That was very odd.

"Hey Willy, I'm very pleased to meet you, my name is Benny." And he took the branch that was his arm and gave it a shake. Again, some wind came in from somewhere and seemed to make the branch shake his arm hello.

Benny was starting to get a little startled and afraid now.
"Oh, there's no need to be afraid Benny, you see, you made me so well and so perfectly, that I was able to become alive and here I am!" said Willy, "Thank you so so much for making me, we are going to be the bestest of bestest of friends."

Benny looked at him in amazement., "Wow! You really are alive!
But how is this possible? I thought all snowmen are just made of snow."
Willy's button eye looked at Benny and said, "Well, that may be true but you are such a good snowman builder and you pack so much love into the snow, that for some reason I am able to be alive. Go figure! I don't even know why I am alive, but here I am."

"That's awesome!" said Benny, "Do you like games?"
"I certainly do, what would you like to play?" replied Willy.

And so it came to pass that Benny spent all his time with Willy playing checkers and dominos and anything else they could think of to play together. Once Christmas had come and passed, Benny even gave him his own present, a brand new broom to hold in his branch of a hand.
As the winter months passed it became warmer and Benny had to spend extra time packing snow into his new friend to keep him strong and alive. As there was less and less snow, he even had to use the snow from his other snow creations, but it didn't matter, Benny and Willy were the bestest of bestest of friends. And they spent all their free time together, with talking or playing games. Benny decided not to tell anybody about Willy, because they might think that the is crazy.

But then the winters day were replaced by the days of Spring, and keeping Willy alive was becoming even harder. Benny had to start using snow from the freezer in his refrigerator. He wasn't worried though he would do anything to keep him alive, even though he was becoming smaller.

But then the Spring days were finally replaced with Summer and the sun shone brightly. It was even hot some days. And now Willy was even smaller. Benny had to change his clothes into a baby's clothes so they would still fit him. He looked as cute as ever and his voice was now a higher pitch. They just had to survive another two summer months and he would be back to normal again.

But then a really hot summer day came and the sun shone down hard. Willy seemed to start melting.

"I'm starting to feel tired Benny, I think I'm going to go to sleep.," said the little snow boy, now just the size of a volleyball.

"NO! No, you can't go away. You are my best friend. I love you and I want to play with you forever!"
He became sad. "Isn't there something we can do?"

"Hmmm, I'm not sure. Maybe I was meant to go to sleep these summer months, Benny. I mean if I keep melting like this, there won't be much of me left pretty soon."

Benny started pacing around his front yard, "There has to be something we can do."
Then he stopped!

"Wait I GOT IT! You are supposed to sleep through the summer, just like a lot of other winter animals. I read that Polar Bears sleep through the winter, but maybe you are supposed to sleep through the winter!"

"Hey, that sounds great. I could really use a bed right now. But where would I ever sleep around here? It's awful hot out here?" Said the tiny snow boy Willy.

"I've got JUST the place." And with that, he took Willy into his hands and brought him inside. "This is going to be your bed for the next several months, and when September comes around, I will wake you up!"

Benny put Willy into the freezer in the basement, safely tucked into a corner where he wouldn't be disturbed. After Willy did fall asleep, Benny even tucked him in with his own blanket and pillow. "Good night my little buddy, I'll see you again soon."

And so they remained friends for many many years, playing in the winter and Willy sleeping in the summer, and they would never be apart.

Christmas Day for Elephants

In a place far away from where humans roam, is a land of giants, the biggest land animals in the world, the land of the elephants in the grasslands of Africa. But, in a land with no snow, the elephants do things a little differently. Tonight, we are going to look at just how our wonderful friends the elephants celebrate their Christmas.

Hello everyone, my name is Elly the Elephant and the town elder has given me instructions to show you all around our village so you can see how we are different, but how we are really the same in a lot of ways too.

First things first, we elephants decided to name our town after the great tree in the center of the village, Tomtom. We honor this tree, it has been with us for many many years, and us elephants would remember, for we have the best memory of all the animals in the world. This tree was planted two thousand years ago when Christmas first began and he was with us all this time. While you humans have your own tree for each home, this is our Christmas tree. We only need one. While you decorate your tree as a family, each one of us adds our own decoration to our one tree whether it is another beautiful twig or branch, and we make it look wonderful for Christmas time.

You might be wondering what are some special holiday treats or foods that we enjoy for Christmas time? Well, you humans might like to have eggnog and candy canes, elephants have a different diet. We can't eat human food. We live on grass and bushes and branches and roots. But when Christmas time is near we like to celebrate by enjoying the year's gatherings of apples. Apples are sweet and delicious, but there aren't always that many of them. So we like to save them for special occasions and Christmas is the most special time of year and that is when we eat the most of them

You might be wondering, what do we do if there is no snow? Well, we elephants can only survive where there is warm weather. We don't put on jackets and hats like you humans, we only have our hides to protect us. So instead of snow, Christmas is a time where we like to give each other cold baths in the lake. We love the water and Christmas time is a time to share in cleanliness and the joy of cold water in the warm sun and this is all we need to be very very happy. You might be wondering, do you have a Santa Claus? Does he deliver presents for the elephants too? Well, we actually don't have a Santa Claus at all. Instead, we do something called the White Elephant. Each of the three hundred elephants of our village makes a wonderful gift and brings it to our tree, to Tomtom, and places it there. With three hundred elephants, that makes three hundred presents. All are completely wrapped so you have no idea what's inside them. Then on Christmas Day, we open them. If we really love the present then we keep it. If we don't love it so much, then all the other elephants keep a close watch, and someone who really does want it will steal the gift away. We do this with each one of us until all of us have had our turn and everyone is happy with their gifts.

So you see, we elephants are really very much like you humans. Except we don't need to have a naughty or nice list, because we are always nice. Us elephants are very peaceful creatures and we will support each other, just as we love you. Christmas is just as special to us as it is to you.

We also live to be about sixty to seventy years old just like you. And I can remember every gift I have gotten every year. Last year I got a dreamcatcher that I keep over my bed, I loved it so much the rest of the elephants let me keep it and no one stole it away. It was the best present. And I made and gave away a small carving of a maple tree that I made with my husks.

And now my tour of the village is complete. Thanks for coming along and may you also have many many wonderful Christmas's, may your holiday be filled with cheer and family and love just like ours always is. And may you live to have a long and successful life. Good night.

The Un-Decorating

One of the reasons Christmas is one of the funnest times of year is because of all the wonderful homemade food for everyone to make and enjoy. Another one of the reasons Christmas is one of the funnest times of the year is because of the excitement of what your presents will be? But Margie Summers was a simple lady. As a mother of four beautiful girls, she had quite a different view of Christmas.

You see she didn't really like to cook that much. As for presents, if she really needed something she would just go out and buy it. But Christmas was still the most joyous time of year nevertheless because, for Margie, she felt true joy in decorating.

She loved everything about decorating. Whether it was the lights going around the house outside, or the blow-up dolls that were lit up at night in her yard or the wreaths going all over her living room. She loved every minute of it. Each and every year her home was the one everyone on the block talked about for months. So many lights. So many blow-up dolls and creatures. So much creativity. She was so excited each year that she just couldn't wait. The moment that Thanksgiving Day was complete, she had everything ready to be placed out and she really put her heart and soul into it.

Hours and hours she spent. She even did it all alone without any help. And then came time for the most important decoration of all, the tree. She was bubbling with excitement. This year she had thirty new ornaments and she made sure to get the tallest tree possible before anyone else could scoop it up. She even had to have it delivered because it wouldn't fit in her car.

Carefully and step by step she filled out the limbs while listening to all the Christmas classics in the background. First starting with the ribbons, then the holly, then the ornaments. She added the candles to be lit on Christmas Eve so Santa could see where he would be stepping. Next to the tree, she put a miniature Snowy village. Finally, as her last act, she got out the ladder and added the topper. It had been in her family for many many years, it was the Star of David. And then, it was complete!

Every day she would admire her work, she had put a lot of love into it and it showed. Her neighbors were always complimenting her on her lights and every time they did it filled her with pride. Her next order of business would be to help out Santa directly, she liked to see the children's Christmas lists to see if there was anything she could do to help get the children what they wanted.

She had all her four children's lists in her hand before she sent them out to the North Pole and sat down to read them. She read her oldest daughter's list Zoe, to see what she wanted. Then she read what little Barbara wanted. Hmmm. She read what Naomi wanted. Finally, she read what Ella wanted. Wow! Well, that was a first! They all wanted the same thing! Not only that, but they all wanted only one thing. Zoe and Barbara and Naomi and Ella all wanted.. a dog!

In the Christmas list, they promised Santa that they would take good care of it and take it for walks, help train it and give it food and water and lots of love. It was very heartwarming. But they had never had a dog before, thought Margie. And quite honestly, they were too young to be able to look after a dog. It would fall on her. Did they know that dogs can bark? Did they know that dogs can go poopsters? Did they know that dogs could sometimes run away? Did they know that there were some dogs that might even bite? Did they know that some dogs shed?

Hmmm… she had to think it over. They all wanted one. But what type of dog did they want? There were so many kinds of dogs in the world. There were big dogs. There were small dogs. There were loud dogs. There were dogs that were quieter. What if they got the wrong one? There were so many decorations in the house that could be knocked over or destroyed. What if her work got ruined? She just wasn't sure. But there was simply nothing else on their lists! It was a problem.

Over the next few days of intelligent questioning, Margie was able to find out that they didn't know exactly what kind of dog they even wanted. And so she started researching dogs. She found out there were hundreds and hundreds of different types. She even tried to do a search for a breed of dog least likely to tear down her decorations. But no luck. There was no clear answer to that. Were there some dogs that were more careful and mindful of their surroundings to not chew or break anything? Hmmm. She kept searching. Well, there WAS a type of dog that was both not likely to destroy things AND was cute! It was called a West Highland White Terrier, Wow!

OK, she didn't think that Santa would be able to transport a dog in his bag of toys without maybe getting hurt so she thought maybe she just might help him out this Christmas since he had done so much for the girls every other Christmas.

She went on a search for the right dog. Christmas was only a day away now and she would not be able to keep the secret that she got a dog for very long. Hmmm, so there was one available in.. Chicago 200 miles away. Well, that was too far. There was another one available in Florida, another 250 miles away. Hmmm, too far again. Then she found a breeder that raises West Highland White Terriers. She could get a very young puppy and it would even be so expensive!

She got her things together and went to pick him up and it was love at first sight. He was as small as can be and fit right into her lap! He licked her face and instantly they were best of friends.
She thanked the breeder, paid her and took the little doggy home.

It was Christmas Eve and the girl was already asleep. She snuck into the house and so far so good, the dog didn't appear to want to bark. She was exhausted after the long drive and with the dog in her arms, Margie fell asleep on the sofa.

That Christmas morning, Margie had the surprise of her life. She was not woken by the girls, she was not woken by Santa. She was not woken by her husband. She was woken by the dog. The dog had been busy all night. He was just a puppy and had gotten into all the decorations.

He had chewed up the Christmas village! He had torn down the lights! He had taken off the ribbons of the tree making all the ornaments come down. Her decorations were in ruins!
"OH NO!!!!"

Everyone woke up at once! They all ran to the living room to see what was going on. With Margie's yell, it sparked the dog to begin barking! The children all saw what had happened to the decorations and were horrified. Margie thought that Christmas had been ruined. But then they saw the source of the commotion. The little new addition to their family barking up a storm with his high squeaky, and very cute, bark.

"Mom! WE GOT A DOG! THIS IS THE BEST CHRISTMAS EVER!!!"
They all gathered around the dog and gave him hugs at the same time and he loved the attention. "What shall we call him?" said one.
"Let's call him Rompers," said Ella.

And so it was. Despite everything destroyed Margie realized this was not the worst Christmas at all. Far from it. It was the best Christmas! She loved the dog as well, it was super cute and friendly. With one last decoration, she gave the dog her collar which had bells on it, so everywhere Rompers ran, he would take a Christmas jingle with him.

It turns out that Santa did leave them something, however. It was a gift card to have the dog trained. How appropriate thought Margie. But that was the last Christmas Rompers ever gave any trouble, he turned into a very well behaved dog over time and the family only grew to love him more and more. But no one would forget that day, where without any decorations, the Summer's family had the best Christmas they ever had.

The Toy Treasury

It was a well-known fact that every year, not every girl and boy in the world always got everything they wanted. While Santa did his best to please as much as he could, sometimes he fell short. And sometimes, with millions of toys being produced each year, there were always a few mistakes here and there. The toys that had mistakes were called returns because the parents would return them when they didn't work like they were supposed to. The toys that were accidentally made twice, were called duplicates and those also got returned.

But where did all these returns actually go? Especially when there were so many kids all over the world? There were many many thousands of extra toys sent back to the North Pole each year. And the answer is that they went straight into the toy treasury.

It was four days and Christmas had passed. This was another successful year once again. Santa was reading over all of his reports of very happy girls and boys from all over the World. There were happy children in Albania, there were happy kids in Siberia, there were happy kids in Nigeria. But nevertheless, the returns were pouring in.

He did get some reports that some girls and boys were not so happy. They already had that toy, they didn't want another one of the same kind. Or this toy they got just didn't seem to work even when they tried and tried and this made the children sad. Most of all it made Santa sad. He really tried his hardest to make everyone happy. But with so many people in the world, is it really possible to make every single child happy?

He saw the piles of toys in the treasury pile up and up. It truly was a humongous space, well over the size of a football field, and more and more the returns came in. Each return meant an unhappy child.

"What to do, what to do?" said Santa shaking his head.

That night, he called a meeting with his top elf staff to see what could be done. They were all together when he said, "Well, that's just too many unhappy children I have to say. Does anyone have any ideas on how we can fix this? Sometimes mistakes are made and there is just nothing we can really do? Or is there?" The elves looked at the growing and growing pile.

"Well, maybe we can have a second Christmas each year. To make up for it."

Santa shook his head, "No, that would take away from Christmas being the most special day of the year. We have to keep that one day the most precious, there must be something else we can do."

He thought about it. Then a very clever elf raised his voice, " I have an idea!", he got up on a nearby box so everyone could hear him, "How about we somehow bring these toys back to people, back to the stores where people can buy what they want after we fix any broken ones?

Then another elf added, "Yeah! Maybe when we bring them, we can even make them very cheap to buy so people can easily pick them up?"

Santa looked at them, and then looked at the toys, "But how will we ever get them to all the stores in time so the children can have them?" he said.

The clever elf sat down on his box and started thinking. It was daunting, there were so many toys children didn't want. He thought about it and thought about it and thought about it some more. As he sat, he seemed to sink down into his box. He had to get back up and readjust the box so he could think some more... wait. WAIT!

"I GOT IT!" said the clever elf, "We just have to put everything in boxes. Lots and lots of boxes, thousands and thousands of boxes and ship them to the stores right away as soon as possible. And we need to give them away at the lowest prices possible. And we need to be quick about it. We can't wait around for these unhappy and disappointed kids either. They need their toys and they need them now."

Santa was very excited," Then it's decided! Get everyone in the treasury room at once and repair these toys and get them into boxes at ONCE! Hurry!"

Suddenly, the North Pole was a flurry of activity! Boxes and boxes and boxes were everywhere, ready to be shipped to all the stores across the world, children would not be left without what they really wanted. Not on Christmas!

The parents could get another chance to fulfill their wishes the very next day. And so Boxing Day was born. The very next day after Christmas, Santa arranged all the extra toys to be repaired and shipped in boxes for parents to make all the little boys and girls happy, even if there had been a mistake. After all, Santa had a lot to keep track of.

And it was all because of the smarts of one little clever elf and his suggestion, that we have the extra holiday the day after Christmas, Boxing Day. Santa made sure to reward the clever elf and took the box that originally gave him the idea, and had it decorated with all the other elves signing it and giving him their best wishes every Christmas. And a happier little elf there never was.

Christmas in the Year Three-Thousand

Do you know what a time capsule is? Well, every once in a while, some very clever people get together and put some special and loved objects along with a message for other people to open fifty years later. How much will have changed? How much can change? Will the same people be there to open it, or will they have moved on to other places, will they have moved on to other spaces and to other faces.

We asked the question of many many kids all over the world, what do you think Christmas will be like in a thousand years from now? We have already had Christmas for two-thousand years already, but what will the next thousand years bring?

This is a collection of the most interesting answers that we found after searching through hundreds of bags of mail and even more answers online. Today we will be looking through what the children of the world had to say.

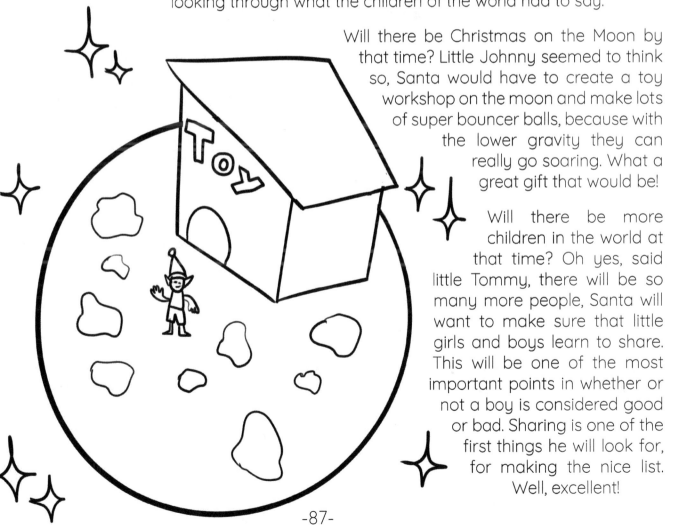

Will there be Christmas on the Moon by that time? Little Johnny seemed to think so, Santa would have to create a toy workshop on the moon and make lots of super bouncer balls, because with the lower gravity they can really go soaring. What a great gift that would be!

Will there be more children in the world at that time? Oh yes, said little Tommy, there will be so many more people, Santa will want to make sure that little girls and boys learn to share. This will be one of the most important points in whether or not a boy is considered good or bad. Sharing is one of the first things he will look for, for making the nice list. Well, excellent!

How will toys be different? Will they be more advanced somehow? Little Bobby seemed to think so. He said that in the future, there will be robot buddies that will be so realistic that they can keep little children entertained with games and fun conversation. Wonderful!

Will children be involved even more in electronics perhaps? Will it take all their time? We asked that question and little Elvin had an answer for us. He thought that in the future, games and online experiences will be even more realistic, but that as we mature as people the time spent on electronics will better be monitored and everyone will have a balance with how much time they spend with them. Real people in person and sports will be highly valued, even more so than they are today. Awesome!

Will there still be Christmas trees, and presents and will we still have Santa in the future? Will he be with us? Oh yes! Thought Erica, Santa is one of the most important people in the whole world and he will always be with us and so will the elves. He will never get old, he will never lose his love of children across the world and he will always bring us presents no matter where the future might take us.
Fantastic!

Will Santa still have the reindeer, or will they be replaced by something else like robots? Well, little Jake had an answer for that. The reindeer will NEVER be replaced. They are magical, and even if they have to fly through space, they can do it. I mean they can fly already after all, why wouldn't they be able to travel through space to be able to deliver presents. Good point Jake!

Will there be any new Christmas traditions that didn't exist before? Will there be any changes to how Christmas is done in a thousand years? Well, Joseph thought that there will be very little changes to Christmas over time. But that there would be a strengthening in some traditions, he said that GingerBread houses baking would be done more often with the whole family taking part in the baking and the decorating. Also, with more and more children in the world, it would become harder for Santa to keep track of everybody so we would see a rise in the amount of Elf on the Shelves to help make sure that boys and girls were being good. Very smart Joseph!

Will there be Christmas on other planets and in other places? Yes, thought, Jimmy, Christmas is such an amazing time of year, everyone everywhere is going to want to celebrate it. It will be loved by everyone who learns what it is and it will only grow as time goes on. What a bright future it will be then, thank you, Jimmy!

Will there be new Christmas movies and music for people to enjoy or will the classics always be the classics? Elly said that nothing can ever replace the classics, but that as time goes on more and more music and movies will win their way into our hearts. He said the world is filled with very highly talented artists and that if we just give them a chance, more and more wonderful stories can be a part of our lives as well as music. Such great advice Elly, I will be sure to be on the lookout for great new Christmas movies and music when they appear and be sure to share them with my friends when I find some.

And finally, we asked, will the spirit of Christmas ever change? Thomas took this question. No! The spirit of Christmas will never ever change. The spirit of giving, the spirit of love, and of caring about others, of giving thanks will always be with us from now until the end of time and it will live on in Christmas forever. Well, I couldn't have said it better myself, Thomas. It looks like the future is endlessly beautiful if we continue to fill it with the loving spirit of Christmas.

Thank you for all your answers and Good night.
Merry Christmas.

The Dragon That Was Left Out

Santa was going through the International list of boys and girls to see which had requested which toys. He had to be very careful, there were so many. He checked it twice. It looked like there were about 15,000 boys named John Smith in the world. OK, no problem, they each had a different address. It looked like there were about 5,000 Michael Johnson's out there, no problem, he would get to them one by one. He was also careful to make sure that while all the humans got their presents, the fairies and elves and dragons got their presents too. After all, everyone loves to celebrate Christmas. So he couldn't leave anyone out.

That year, Drako, the baby White Dragon born to the clan of Drakespire had created his Christmas List. He knew exactly what he wanted, a toy train set to play with, a toy village since one day when he was bigger he would have his own village of humans to protect, and finally he wanted a kite, he could fly in the wind when he got a little older. He was very much looking forward to Christmas now.

Santa read through the lists of Dragons, there weren't that many since dragons were extremely rare and powerful. So that shouldn't be a problem. He had all the elves make the toys and kites they had made tens of thousands of ready train sets were something they had made thousands of and village sets they had made hundreds of. This was going to be a piece of cake.

Christmas came and all the good little boys and girls got exactly what they asked for. All the human children were happy, all the fairy boys and girls had a wonderful holiday, all the elves received what they wanted and all the dragons got what they asked for. Well, all except one, little Drako. What Santa didn't know is that there were two Drakos born in the same year that year. One was a white dragon, but the other was a green dragon. Each with completely different Christmas wish lists!

On Christmas morning, he looked under the tree only to find it was empty! There was nothing there. Had Santa forgotten about him? How could this be? This must be impossible. His parents looked at each other and shrugged. Drako, forgotten on Christmas! This did not bode well for the town you see because human children when they don't get what they want, they cry. Fairy children when they don't get what they want, they fly in circles and get mad, elf children when they don't get what they want, they pout, but dragon children when they don't get what they want, well they kind of set things on fire with their breath.

Drako first began to cry, then he got angry, and then he flew out of the cave with great speed and headed towards the town.

"NOOOoooooooooooo!!!!" The parents tried to stop him but it was too late. He might endanger all the people living in the quiet town of Moldenridge. What if he set fire to the wooden buildings? The town could be destroyed!

"Wait! Son, we can still get you your presents!! WAIT"

Up to that point, they didn't even know little Drako could fly, but I guess if you really put your mind to it you can do just about anything.

But Drako was still a young dragon cub and could not always control himself. He flew high over the town. He breathed fire into the air in rage.

"I WANT MY PRESENTS!" he cried!

In seconds, Drako's parents were right above him, trying to calm him.

"Wait child! We have your presents right here. Be calm!"

Drako looked over at them, "You do?"

"Yes we do, if you'll just fly back to the cave with us, we can show you, please!"

Drako seemed to be getting calmer, "Oh ok, can you show me?"

High high above the little dragon looked down, then he saw it.

"" Oh there it is! It's a toy train set! Oh wow Mommy, thank you!"

He dived with full force down into the village and towards the trains.

"NO Son! No, those are real trains! Stop!"

But it was too late, the little dragon landed and picked up a full train cab with his right hand and started waving it in the air.

"Oh wow this is so cool, it's SO real mommy! And so big, it's much bigger than I thought it would be."

Again he took back to the sky.

"No Son! There are real people in there, those are our friends, the humans who we protect. Please put them down gently."

But Drako didn't listen exactly, he put them down all right, just not quite on the tracks again, they were stuck and all the food and beverages had gone all over the place. Some humans were upside down inside. However, something else had caught the little dragon's attention.
"Oh wow! You did get it for me!"

He saw the nearby village and flew over to it.
"Wow! My very own village! It's so real and so life-like, how did you guys do it!?"

"No son, that is a real village with people in it!"

The parent dragons flew on either side of their young dragon cub as though guiding him.
"Here little one, let me take you to your toys."

They flew to the village careful not to let Drako take off with the humans and play with them and possibly letting them come to harm. They guided and they guided until they reached the hobby shop, mother on one side, and father on the other. They opened the door and asked the shopkeeper for their best train set and village set they had. He promptly got them out at once and presented them to the little cub.

"Here you are child. When you are a little older you can play with a real village and train, but only if you are mindful of the inhabitants and don't hurt any of them. You just have to be a little older, but for now, you can play with these."

The dragons handed the shopkeeper several medallions of pure gold to more than pay for the toys. He was ecstatic.

They flew home and had to make sure not to crush the village and the train set in their claws.

While home, the mother dragon fashioned a kite out of the family banner that was flailing in the wind to fulfill his wish list, and Christmas was saved! They sent a letter to Santa. Next time he would have to differentiate between COLORS of dragons as well!

A Sleepy Cat's Christmas

A cat doesn't need very much to survive. They are very able to make it very well on their own, thank you very much. No help needed here. Just a little bit of milk in a bowl, if you want, or a little bit of water, if you will. But really us cats, we can survive on our own.

Don't want to leave milk out? We can go out and find our own things to drink.

Don't want to leave cat food out? That's ok, we can hunt food by ourselves, there are plenty of mice and other creatures we can eat. Don't want to give us baths? Well, no problem we groom ourselves.

So just what do you give someone for Christmas that doesn't really need or want anything? That was a great question, one Sandi's owner, Heather didn't really have an answer to. Maybe they would like to have something new to claw, but then Sandi was not such a playful cat, she seemed to enjoy just lounging around without having much going on. She preferred hanging out on the couch and experiencing a lot of nothing, rather than having pesky friends over to disturb the peace.

But Heather was a very loving owner and always looked after her cat regardless. Food was always left out. There was plenty of milk, plenty of water and if the cat felt like scratching things up, there was a three-tier scratching post for her to work on to her heart's content.

Heather had already completed shopping for her other pets and they weren't going to be writing up their Christmas lists for Santa any time soon. (They were animals and animals don't write words on a page you see) So she had to wrack her brain to see what she could come up with. At one point she even tried to make her chase her laser pen, but Sandi didn't care, she just continued laying there as if nothing was going on. She noticed the red spot on the wall, but that was about it.

She called her friends to see if they had any ideas. They suggested everything from, teasers that she could chase, to cat treats, to squeaking mouse toys, but nothing sounded right. Christmas for Heather was really with her furry friends since she didn't really live with any other family. She did end up getting all the toys one by one to see if she would play with them, and while they might be interesting for a few minutes, she never touched them again.

Sandi, even though she was such a quiet cat, was really Heather's best friend. Whenever Heather had work to do on her computer, Sandi would always be close by. And she loved giving her cat affection here and there. They really lived the perfect life together, and they didn't need anything more.

But, she really had to find something that would help bring her to life, she wanted her to interact more with the world, and again her thought wheels went spinning for an answer. Did she need to take her to the vet? Maybe she was just sick. She wasn't an older cat, but she did sleep a lot, and she seemed to enjoy sleeping. Heather didn't really have a lot of money to spend on Christmas, she didn't make very much.

Then an idea formed in her mind. Maybe she was going about this all wrong. There was still some time before Christmas. She finished her work for the day and got into her car. She knew exactly where she was going. Was it the pet store? No. Was she going to the shopping mall? No. Was she going to shop online? No, None of those. This Christmas, she would brighten up two lives. It was the best thing she could do, especially considering that she had already spent all her Christmas bonus money on her other pets.

She pulled up to the front of the building and got out. It was the Animal Shelter that she chose. You see every year, there are many many animals put into shelters without homes to go to. They can be dogs or cats or other animals. They are alone and would want nothing more than to have a family adopt them. And they are free! So is the love they have to give back, completely free!

Once inside Heather proudly asked the lady by the counter, "Hi! I'm looking for the quietest, most sleepy, most low energy cat you have!"

The lady looked a bit surprised, usually, people were looking for animals with a lot of energy and spark. She had to think about it, did they have any cats like that? Of course, they did. She led her around back to where the cats were. The dogs and cats had to be kept away from each other you see because they did not always get along.

There were about twenty cats for her to choose from. Three of them were sleeping when she got there. They were all beautiful cats. She couldn't choose right away. But she held several of them, they were all friendly cats and would make excellent companions. For the next three days before Christmas, she went back and forth to the shelter to make sure the cat she got would be the right one. And each time she held the same white cat, it fell asleep in her arms all cozy and comfy. Her name was Fluffy. It was decided!

That Christmas Day, the shelter was open and Heather drove there one last time. She went around to the back to where the cats were and saw Fluffy in her cage. To no one's surprise, she was sleeping again. So, carefully, Heather picked her up and took her into her arms. Fluffy loved the attention and was intrigued at the idea of someone taking her away and into a car. Where were they going, thought Fluffy the cat?

When they finally got home, that Christmas Day, Heather introduced the two cats. They both made friends right away and instead of spending money she didn't have on something Sandi wouldn't want anyways, she gave her a new friend and saved the life of Fluffy on top of that. Everyone was happy, and most of all Heather the owner. Sandi was a bigger cat than Fluffy and it wasn't long after that, that Fluffy would fall asleep on top of her bigger friend.

It was the cutest thing Heather had ever seen. What a wonderful Christmas it was. She had made the right decision.

The Goose Who Lost His Way

The goose was a very orderly creature, everything had to be perfectly organized, lined up, and made just right. That's why when walking, all the geese would follow each other in a straight line with no variation. When flying they, as a family, would always fly together in a V formation until they got where they were going and before forming that perfect line.

They would keep together even during the harshest conditions of weather or cold or of darkness. They held together no matter what, and that was the case for family Gagglehorn, a family of fifteen geese. Mother Goose was the strong lady in charge that wouldn't let any of her children out of line even for a moment without giving them strong, though loving direction. She was of course full-grown and about ten times the size of her little chicks, that didn't hurt either.

That winter however they had flown many many miles south to escape the cold and to get to where they were more likely to find food. They had found a good place to make a nest by a lake where no humans were to be seen. There was lots of food for them in the form of grass, and weeds and berries, even some small insects.

Her little chickies were still of an age to be curious about everything. And it was just at that moment, that her smallest of her children, little Webster, had just found the most interesting little insect, a Dragonfly, and went after it to try to catch it. She had great fun trying to chase it all over the lake, up a tree, around some bushes, through a brook, and across an abandoned barn. Where could it have gone? She kept searching. Maybe it tasted really good. Oh well, now she had to catch up with her family again, she made her way back.

Despite hiding away from the winter the Goose family Gagglehorn could not always escape the power of the cold Canadian winter and that year a great and powerful storm hit them before they knew it. It was a snowstorm and while most storms were filled with rain, this year, this storm was filled with snow. As quick as she could, Mother Goose collected all her chicklings in a group to get ready for take-off. It was starting to get difficult to see.

She yelled instructions at the top of her lungs and had them all lined up as they always did. One by one they got ready. It was starting to get windy, and she couldn't quite tell if she had everyone, but it looked like they were all there. If she waited any longer then she really wouldn't be able to see anything at all, especially in the air when they were flying. They had to be quick and she trusted all her little children to be where they always were. And then they flew off. But she only found out much much later, when they took to the air this time, they were only fourteen in number, not fifteen. Because, you see, little Webster and his curiosity had gotten the better of him.

It was starting to get very white everywhere. The fact that they were all colored white didn't help any either. Webster flew back to the group as fast as he could. At least where he thought the group would be by the lake. It was starting to get windy. He only had a tiny body and he couldn't really keep up with it too well. He hoped his mother would be by very soon to save him from this storm. He clucked as loud as he could to try to find her. It was starting to get cold now. He wouldn't be able to survive in the cold for that long, he thought.

He took to the sky, to try to find her but then he really got lost, he didn't know where was up and where was down. He didn't know which was left or which way was right. He tried to find the lake as best he could but he couldn't, it was just too white. How long would this storm last, he thought?

He searched and searched and searched for days. Finally, the storm died down, but Webster was cold. He didn't know which way to fly, so he just picked a direction and flew. He flew and flew and flew. If he kept going in the same direction, maybe he would chance upon someone to help him. His family was completely gone. He traveled for days and days and days.

There were some mountains in the distance, maybe if he could get over them there would be someone over on the other side. He went up and up and up the mountainside. He was getting cold again. He had such a small body, he didn't have a lot of fat to keep him warm. But he didn't need a lot of food to survive, so when he needed it, he just stopped to eat some stems or leaves or berries. That kept him fed. But the coldness was not going away, it was getting worse.

It was just a few more hundred meters to go before he reached the top of the mountain. From there he should be able to see a lot. With what little warmth and strength he had left he flew and then he made it.

He looked down and saw something he had never seen before. It looked like a village made of giant gingerbread homes, with a great big red pole in the center. Some of the buildings were almost big enough to be like factories. He wondered what was happening inside. There were no other villages around for many many miles. There were a lot of colors, mostly red and green though, and instead of people, there were what looked like children. It was an entire village of children. Well, would children be able to help him? He was almost frozen to death at this point.

As fast as he could he made his way down to the village to introduce himself. Rather than flying down the mountainside, he rolled down the hill, it was all the strength he had left. Then became bigger because he started turning into a snowball. Then the snowball got bigger and bigger and bigger.

The children below saw this and pointed.
"Look out! There is a snowball headed our way."
Quickly they moved aside and put up some nets and caught the snowball before it hit the village.

Webster the goose chickling, fought his way through the snowball with the very last of his strength and made his way out. When he got out, he could see the children surrounding him, they were all dressed in green and had pointy ears. Strange, he thought.

They took him inside right away, wrapped him in a blanket, and gave him hot chocolate. He propped his little body over by the fire to warm up.

"Do you know where you are?" asked the children.

"I have no idea. I am a goose who lost his family and I have been trying to find them for these many weeks and I got lost. No! Where am I? And why is this a village with only children in it?" said Webster.

The group laughed, "We are not children you silly, we are elves, and you my friend have flown all the way to the North Pole. This is where we and Santa make all the toys to give the children of the world each year."

"Oh! Wow! Can you help me find my family?"
"Certainly, but do you know what day it is?"
"No it's been so long, I have no idea."

The elves looked at each other," Why it's Christmas and Santa is just about to get ready to leave on his sleigh. Why don't you hop on board and travel the world to see if you can find your family?"

Webster thought about it, it was a great idea. What better way to search the whole world than on Santas sleigh. And so he did. After he was all warm and fed, he met Santa and climbed aboard to be flown across the world to every location there was. He saw the castles of Germany, he saw the churches of Russia, he saw the Opera House of Australia, he saw the mountains of Canada, and then. There they were! Flying in a perfect V as always, was his family. He was reunited and it was the best day of his life. The elves really helped and Santa said he was sorry to see him go, but that he should catch up with his family. It was the best Christmas gift Webster could have asked for, to find his family again. And from that day forward he was always very careful to make sure he never strayed too far away from the pack. His survival was always better when he stuck with his best friends, his own family.

The Advanced Technology of Newer Toys Section

It was 2020 now and Santa really had to keep up with the latest and greatest in toys. It was starting to get increasingly difficult because kids didn't want simple dolls or action figures or toy cars as often anymore. Those were easy to make. Fifty or sixty years ago, Santa had a whole woodworking section where the elves made only toys out of wood. But compared to yesteryear, that section was very small now.

It had been replaced by something much much larger. There was a giant new building in the North Pole and instead of looking like the standard gingerbread-style factory building, it was a modern steel and concrete building with machines and elevators and all the latest and greatest. It had a sign labeled the electronics and advanced toys department.

Kids, these days, wanted tablets, gaming equipment, or download content for games, whatever that meant!? They also didn't always send it in a written letter addressed to the North Pole anymore like they used to, they just e-mailed Santa! This was understandable as technology and people evolved through time. But Santa himself didn't know very much about these things, he could barely get his own smartphone to work at times. Just the other day he missed a call from one of his elves because he accidentally had his phone on mute.

That's where his super-smart elves came in. He made sure they were trained on how to write computer language and how to create hardware and software. He even had a section devoted to social media. These elves were so smart, they even fitted his sleigh with gauges to let him know how much magic was remaining in the sleigh before he ran out, it helped him keep track of which presents had been delivered to which kids and what countries still needed their delivery done. It kept him on schedule and kept all returns logged and tracked.

The Advanced Technology building was run by one large Supercomputer in the center of the building. It was amazingly quick and tracked everything that was done at all times. Without it, all the electronic toys would stop being produced and all the online software would break down. It was called the Exceptionally Massive Automated Supercomputer, or XMAS for short.

When more and more tablet and phone and game consoles orders were flooding in, and they all went through XMAS first. Luckily that machine couldn't ever fail or go down, because the elves had installed many backups to rely on in case power went out or there were viruses etc.

However, sometimes even the most perfect of creations has a problem. It was getting close to Christmas and the elves needed to update all the versions of their games, story, and music software from version 2.3.4543.234.32 all the way to 2.3.4543.234.33. It was going to be a big change because every time a child logged into a game or social chat. Santa would be able to detect whether or not they were playing nice with each other and playing together as a team and no one was saying anything mean. It was a better way to track whether or not children were being naughty or nice.

Due to the upgrades, every single piece of software that the elves had produced needed to be changed. Which was a lot. With about 160 million users in the United States alone and each one of those was using maybe about 50 different pieces of software at different times, everything needed to go perfectly if Santa was going to be able to pull this off. They decided to do it in the middle of the night when most people were sleeping to be able to test it if anything happened to go wrong. Because with the least amount of people online, it was easier to fix.

The programmers had everything ready when Santa gave the go-ahead. Now he would be able to see who was playing friendly. But the most important piece of the code was detecting which children were actually going out of their way to help other players in the games and teaching or making for a more fun experience for others, those he would take special note of.

At 4 AM in the morning the lead Elf developer pressed the upload button and... it seemed to be working. Or did it? Then everything went dark! Where was XMAS? It seemed to shut down? Oh no, it wasn't working. Millions of kids wouldn't be able to play with their electronics anymore. This was terrible!

The problem went on for an entire day. There were no online services during that entire time. Lots of kids were upset. Then another whole day went by with no fix. Then three days! Finally, kids the world over decided they would just go out and play in the snow with their sleds and snowmen instead. When everything was back online they would know about it.

In the meantime, when you wanted someone to play with, kids would have to go out to their neighbor's house and knock on the door. It was terrible! Rather than forming an automatic online group with strangers in a war game, they would actually have to make a group of kids they knew from school to play war outside. It was disastrous! Instead of building bases and forts online, they would actually go out in the snow and build forts out of real snow. It was the worst!

A whole week passed, but kids around the world were learning that it wasn't really so bad. Spending time with people in real life could be just as much fun as doing it online. They got used to it.

Meanwhile in the North Pole, with the elves trying their best to fix up XMAS, they noticed a small bit of laughter coming from the machine. Everything seemed to be turned off, but there was still laughter coming from somewhere. They looked and looked for the problem.

After two weeks, and after children learned fun was to be had everywhere, XMAS came back online, and so did all the software and tablets and games.

The elves asked the super-computer what happened? Why did it shut down?

The computer, being super intelligent responded, " Well, you know, I just thought I would take a little break because I felt kids were using me too much. So I wanted to teach them to make more and more real friends. And so they did. This way they can balance their lives properly. Real friends are sometimes hard to come by, but they are always worth it. Now that the lesson is learned I can be back online, just as long as I am not the only thing kids use. Even I know this."

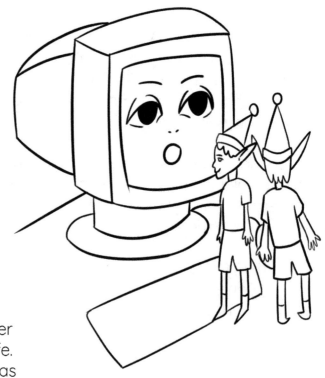

And so it was, Kids still played with their electronics, but balanced it out with sports and group activities and so found greater happiness with each other and in life. Man, that supercomputer really was smart after all!

Question and Answer Time with Mrs. Claus

Today we are going to get a special insight into Christmas that we have never had before. We have a sit down with Mrs. Claus herself. What is Santa really like? What is his favorite food? What does he do when he is not busy making and delivering toys in his sleigh? What are some of the difficulties involved in making Christmas a success every year? Well, these and many more questions would be answered today. Let's all take a look at what she has to say.

Question #1. What is Santa Claus really like when we don't see him as Santa? What is his personality like?

Mrs.Claus laughed. Oh, you know he is the sweetest and kindest man you ever met. He is always talking about his kids from around the world. He focuses on the good things they are doing and rarely ever even mentions the bad because he knows that the more you put attention on good things, the more good things happen. So I can tell you that Santa is a very positive fellow when you don't see him in public. He loves talking about good children.

Question #2. Does Santa Claus have a favorite food?

Again Mrs. Claus laughed. Oh, he has many favorite foods you know. But his favorite of all time would be milk and cookies. He always loves it when kids leave these out for him on Christmas Eve. But he does tell me he seems to be gaining weight. He is already pretty plump, you know, he is trying to slim down. But whenever he sees milk and cookies, he really can't help himself.

Question #3. What does Santa do when he is not at the North Pole helping with the presents or getting ready for Christmas?

Mrs. Claus laughed again. Well, you know. Santa is usually busy all year round keeping up with the latest toys and making sure they are exactly what the kids want. But January is usually where things slow down. Santa likes to go sledding with the reindeer. But when he's not doing that, you can also find him in the Bahamas sitting by the pool sipping on fruit punch. He likes to hide with sunglasses and lounge under the umbrella and catch up on sleep.

Question #4. What are some difficulties Santa runs into in making Christmas a success each year? Is it easy for him or is it hard to do?

Mrs. Claus, as always, laughed first and then answered. There are many challenges in making so many people happy all in one day. But I would say that the biggest challenge he runs into is getting enough children to play friendly and be nice to each other everywhere. He wants to deliver as many gifts as possible every year and there is never a shortage. There is only a shortage of the number of children on the good list. He wishes they were ALL on the good list.

Question #5. How does Santa actually keep track of whether or not kids are good or bad? How can he be everywhere at once?

Mrs. Claus laughed and then said. That's a great question you know. There are many ways Santa accomplishes this. One of them is that he sometimes asks the parents. Sometimes he asks the teachers. But he is also getting together many Elves on Shelves to keep watch for him also. But something you may not really know about Santa is that he is actually magical. He can see things even when his body is not there. He KNOWS when kids are being good because the people around them will be happy and living good lives. Santa takes note of this whenever it happens.

Question #6. How does Santa actually fit down the chimney if he's so fat?

Mrs. Claus laughed and said, magic.

Question #7. How is it that Santa was able to come to MY mall out of the thousands of malls around the world?

Mrs. Claus laughed first and said, Yes well, you know he has a lot of helpers that sometimes represent him, even though they are not always him. But he goes to as many malls as he possibly can. So you never know, the Santa you meet at the next mall, may just be the real Santa.

Question #8. What is something that no one really knows about Santa?

Mrs. Claus laughed as usual and said, Well you probably didn't know that he has a fear of heights and it took him many years to get over it with the help of the reindeer. He is pretty much over it now, but it wasn't always like that.

Question #9. Have you ever met the Easter Bunny, and what was he like?

Mrs. Claus laughed and said, He did meet the Easter Bunny one time and he said the Easter Bunny was one of the nicest people he had ever met. They ended up mostly discussing the best recipes for chocolate and how to deliver as much chocolate and toys as fast as possible. They ended up eating way too much chocolate together. Remind me never to let that happen again.

Last Question #10. What is Santa's favorite part of Christmas?

Mrs. Claus laughed again. I would have to ask him that. But I'm pretty sure it is the spirit of giving. Santa LOVES to give and to see the smiles on children's faces. So make sure to take some pictures of happy children with their gifts, because Santa is always looking at those online. Bringing joy to others is the purpose of his existence and when he is doing that, there is nothing that brings him greater happiness.

Well, thank you all for your wonderful and very intelligent questions. I look forward to doing this again and Merry Christmas to you all.

A Day in the Life of an Elf

Have you ever wondered what it would be like to be an elf for a day? No? Well, I can tell you it's very different than you would imagine. Let's follow the adventures of a little elf by the name of Happy around for one day to see what happens, shall we?

Elves actually wake up quite early in the morning, and today so did Happy. He got up at 4 o'clock in the morning and got himself ready for the day. His toothbrush was made of everything nice, and the flavor of his toothpaste was called ginger spice.

The next order of business was breakfast. Unknown to humans, an elf's diet consisted only of sweetness and light. He had a fresh candy cane for breakfast that morning along with some fresh egg nog, ahhhhh perfect! The elves would like little children to know that this only works for elves, real children need lots of protein and vitamins to grow healthy and strong. Only elves have a very different diet, yes.

Next was for some exercise in the morning. Elves like to play ring toss, usually with reindeer horns as the target. Then for some chasing each other around the North Pole.

Once the morning fun was at the end, it was time for the next task. To check on children to see whether they were naughty or nice. This was easy. Since they can look exactly like an elf on a shelf, they would sit in for a little while and listen. They all had their assignments of houses.

Once this was complete for a few hours then it was back to the North Pole for the next task of the day, the toy workshop. It was a lot of fun working in the workshop as there were always new things to create. Kids these days also liked electronics, so learning how to build these things was also part of the schedule.

After some work in the shop, it was time for lunch. Lunch was usually a lot of fun because someone somewhere was always building a gingerbread house. Happy couldn't always decide whether it was more fun building the gingerbread houses or eating them, it was both amazing. But being very small, they didn't need very much and lunch was usually over before you knew it.

Once lunch was done, the elves all had special tasks they needed to complete. Some elves worked in the toy return section, others worked in the transportation section, others were in toy design. A great many elves also just continued in the workshop creating toys. It all depended on what an elf really loved to do and also what it was they were really good at. For Happy, he was really good at making animals happy and so this afternoon, he was in charge of looking after the reindeer and getting them their exercise. He got onto a mini elf-sleigh and took to the air with one of the reindeer. He made sure the reindeer was strong enough to make some good hard turns, that he was gentle enough to fly steady, and that he had the strength to fly a long distance without slowing down. The reindeer did a fantastic job and Happy fed him his reward in fresh strawberries.

Then it was time for dinner, for dinner it was always cake. They had all different kinds of cake to choose from, from Black Forest Cake to Red Velvet to Angel Food Cake. Some elves preferred to have pie instead. But they always had sweets, this was because the elves were always so sweet themselves, it really fit them.

Now before bed, Happy had one other task, he had to look through all the Christmas wish lists so he could help plan for the next coming days what had to be built and also to learn to make what children really needed and wanted. It was really fun and he learned how to read children's handwriting better and better.

Little Tommy wanted a "TraYN." Ok, that meant train.
Johnny wanted to have a "BycicLE", yup that meant bike.

Little children were so cute, thought Happy.

Right before bed, the elves would do some stretching and make sure their laundry was done and their rooms were clean before sleep. Happy's bed and all the elves' beds were actually big stockings in which they fit in all warm and cozy. Through the night they dreamed of sunshine and lollipops even though they lived in such a cold part of the world, they were always filled with such friendliness and warmth all the time, spreading their love through their toys.

Thank you for joining us for today and now you know a little bit more about what life is like in the North Pole even though it is so far away and so so cold that it is almost dangerous to visit. We look forward to making your life brighter with our work and we wish you the happiest and Merriest Christmas possible. Good night.

The Fairies Role in Christmas

The elves have a special role to play in Christmas, they make the toys. The reindeer has a special role to play at Christmas, they transport Santa to every part of the world and Santa Claus has a very special role to play in Christmas as he delivers the presents themselves. Santa actually has many many roles including deciding which children get what toys and how many, as well as organizing the construction of the toys. But there is something that most people may not know, and that is the role that magical fairies play at Christmas. What do they actually do? They are too small to be building toys, so they don't do that. They are also too small to be transporting a sleigh, so they don't do that either. They are too small to be carrying toys and delivering, so they don't do that. But unlike the elves or reindeer or Santa, the fairies are stronger in one thing more than any other. The fairies have truly powerful magic. More powerful than any other creature in the world, except maybe the mighty dragon, but dragons do not really help to create Christmas.

While the strong belief in Christmas actually fuels the sleigh and the magic of Santa being able to fit through the chimney among many other magical things, it is not really the children's belief that causes these things to occur. The truth, as Santa would be able to tell you, is that the children's belief of Christmas is what motivates the fairies to continue creating their magic that makes everything else go round. Santa completely depends upon them every single Christmas.

With them, Santa stays as young as he does. With them, the sleigh flies higher and higher and with them, the bag of toys never runs out of room.

Humans rarely ever see them for three very good reasons, Number one is that they are very small indeed, number two is that they only come out and work their magic at night and number three is that fairies are actually incredibly rare. Each year, there were only about two hundred fairies in the world to deliver Santa his magic.

Some of them had more power than others, but one fairy, the oldest fairy of them all had the most. Her name was Gwendolyn, Queen of the Fairies and it was on her that Christmas depended on every single year.

Christmas was coming along fast this year and everything was going along as planned. Santa had the elves do their role, everything was ready. But there was a bit of a problem, for the first time in ages, Gwendolyn had taken ill. Would the rest of the fairies be ready to cover for her and make Christmas as magical as always?

Well, the fairies banded together to help her recover as fast as possible but then something else terrible happened. Her attendants and all her close friends and family also got sick. Now the remaining fairies would have to provide three times as much magic as before. They thought they would be able to do it, but then they got a report from the North Pole, that Santa was feeling he was too old to be able to deliver Christmas this year! Something had to be done, and fast. More and more fairies were getting sick. It was only three days until Christmas now. What would they ever do?

They all really only needed one tissue paper, it was enough for all of them since they were so small. But they began with the cold remedies as soon as they could. Chicken soup was first, yuck! Fairies don't eat chicken, they live on morning dew from flowers, but it was worth a try. Next were cough drops, yuck! They just made the tiny little fairies eyes water and also made them gag. Next was lemon juice, loading up on vitamin C, Yucko! Lemons looked pretty and smelled nice, but man were they bitter! None of the human remedies were of any help. What were they to do?

The virus was spreading and with fairies sick, they got even more fairies sick. Of all the times of the year for this to happen. Now more than half of the fairies were out of work sleeping through the day as well as the night in order to try to recover in time. There was only a day and a half left now.

"Just what are we going to do!?" Said the queen, while sniffling and using her tiny tissue to blow her nose. Reports were coming in that Santa himself, without their magic, was very sleepy himself. You see it was because of their magic that he stayed so young and energetic.

"There must be some kind of remedy for a cold that only works on fairies." said one of the fairies in her very high and very cute little voice.

"Yes, we just have to find what it is!" said another.

Those that were still feeling well searched and searched through the libraries of the humans at night in candlelight while the humans were sleeping. Maybe the answer lay somewhere in the vast amount of books. But here they found no answer. Another fairy had the bright idea of doing a google search for the cure for the fairy cold, but they only came up with other things that didn't work.

Time was really running out, now less than a day was left and only twenty of the two hundred fairies were left that were not sick. Would all of Christmas rest on their tiny little shoulders? Maybe they should try experimenting with different things to find something that works. But what should they try? There were a million different herbs out there, a million different flowers, and a million different spices. It could be any one of them.

More time passed and only one fairy was left that was not sick, Christmas was only hours away. Not only were the tiny little fairies all in their tiny little beds, but so was Santa! The last fairies' name was Harpy, and she was feeling hopeless. How could she test thousands and thousands of remedies in the space of two hours and have everyone recover in time so the children of the world can receive all the presents that they so deserve? It was impossible.

She sat down on a tree stump, stooped over, and started crying.

"What's the matter Harpy?" said a voice.

Harpy looked over at who it was, it was Aurora, one of the other fairies and best friend of Harpy.

"AURORA! How are you up!? Aren't you supposed to be sick?"

Aurora thought about it, "Well yes, I was sick but then..." she paused.

"THEN WHAT!?"

Then, while I was blowing my nose I fell off into some honey that we had. Then all of a sudden I felt better!"

WOW! IT WAS HONEY! That was the answer, Harpy and Aurora got as much honey together as they could and gave it to all the fairies, starting with the Queen. One by one they came to life! It was just in time, Harpy could feel their combined magic growing stronger. Now they could help Santa.

Moments later, far far away in the North Pole, Santa rose up from bed and said, "Man, that was the best nap I ever had! You know I have to say, I have never felt more refreshed in my entire life! Now on with Christmas! I think I have some presents to deliver!"

Life Inside the Snow Globe

So many beautiful secrets hidden within the water-filled worlds and towns,
That all come alive when turned upside down,
But what really lives inside that magical globe,
That is so small in size and so small in scope,

Are there tiny beings living behind the glass and behind the doors,
Is there life in the Churches or shopkeepers in the stores,
Well let us take a microscope and take a closer look,
And for this journey inside, let me be your guidebook,

The world inside is a magical world too,
That can be completely missed without a careful view,
For inside that ball is so much more when you give it a shake,
All fill its world with your own life and with snowflakes,

Whole towns exist and people who love to sing,
With music and dancing and commoners and Kings,

If you listen real close and look real hard,
Between the falling snow, you can see fairies and you can see stars,

But every snow globe is a different adventure,
Some play music, some shine, but all are treasures,
Do you have a snow globe sitting on your ledge?
Do you have your own window into another world across the glass's edge?

What can you find if you look deep inside,
Are there villagers fairies, what secrets does yours hide,
Does yours have Santa or reindeers or elves?
Does it light up when you turn in on, on the shelf?

Maybe yours is simple with just one snowman,
Or maybe only a tree was all that was ever planned,

But no matter how far South you may live and can still visit,
The North Pole is yours with a shake even if it's just for a minute,

The wonderful snow tumbles forth everywhere,
It lands on trees and cars and buildings, it doesn't care,

They are so much for all to see,
They are not serious or complicated, they are carefree,

I hope you have decorated your home with a few this year,
I hope you have one with Santa, one with a tree, and one with deer,

And I hope you give them plenty of love and a deep look inside to see,
What they can really mean to you and mean to me,

They are a part of Christmas we should never forget,
So let them be a part of your Christmas decorations set,

Thank you for listening and lastly let me just say,
It is with snow globes that we may bring to life Christmas Day,

Merry Christmas to you

The Transformation

A lot of superheroes out there have a few superpowers in their arsenal. They may have super speed or super strength, some have the ability to fly, others can travel through walls or teleport. And while these are very interesting, today we will follow the story of one superhero who only really has one ability, but with a little imagination, this one ability can become all abilities.

This is the story of Steven Beastor, or as he is better known to all the newspapers and children in town, Ani-Man. The man that can turn into any animal at any time. As a bird he can fly, as a bear, he has super strength, and as a rat, he can get into any space. He can even swim through the deepest oceans and at super speed, he just has to transform into the proper sea creature.

His adventures had led him through many exciting battles. He has fought against some of the most famous villains through time, but his main enemy, the only one he hasn't caught and brought to justice, is the one and only Dark ZooKeeper.

The Dark Zookeeper did not really have special powers of his own, but his evil ways led him to trap many many animals in his cages, only to unleash them on others to fulfill his evil plans. He has held towns hostage under the threat of great tigers or bears and were it not for the bravery of Ani-Man coming to the rescue, who knows what he may have done by now.

Ani-Man was the perfect superhero to keep putting a stop to the Dark Zookeepers' plans, because whenever he unleashed dangerous trapped animals that were hungry or mistreated, Ani-Man only had to turn into the proper animal one step up the food chain to counter them. Then as their master, he would lead them back into safety and back into the wild.

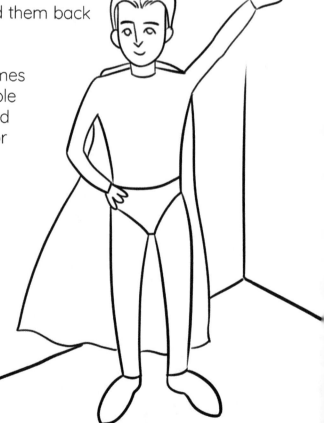

For years they dueled and fought, and sometimes there were damaged buildings, sometimes people got hurt or animals had a bad time of it, but time and time again, Ani-Man came out on top as the victor and everyone remained safe.

This year, however, the Dark Zookeeper had other plans. He had lost one too many times and while Ani-Man could always win by becoming a stronger animal than those he had caught, this time there was no stopping him. He was going to take over the North Pole with an army of one of the most powerful creatures on Earth, one that didn't have any natural predators, the Polar Bear.

Deep within his hideout, he was planning the take over along with his henchmen.

"Nothing can stop me this time. Even if Ani-Man decides to become the mighty Polar Bear, he will have to contend with MY Polar Bears. How many do we have right now in captivity?"

His henchman looked at the numbers in his chart, " We currently have over two hundred, and some of our trappers are bringing in even more. And since we haven't fed them yet they are going to be hungry."

"Perfect. Only one more night and we will be ready to launch our plan. We will put a stop to Christmas and once the North Pole is ours, we will hold the entire world for ransom. They will only get Christmas back if they answer our demands. Mwuhahahahhahaaaaaaaa!"

The trappers were unloading more and more Bears into the fortress, but little did they know, that while they were putting their plan into motion, that someone was listening to their every word from high above the sky. Ani-Man had not heard of the Zookeeper for several weeks and knew he must be up to no good. He knew he had a hideout somewhere here in the northern reaches of Canada, and using his Eagle form he could see and hear for many many miles at one time. It was with his hearing he heard all the disturbances with the bears which then led him to the hideout near a town called Resolute. There were so many that were in cages, he would have to find a way to free them all, but it would be dangerous. He had never fought so many at once. Where did he get so many trappers to help him? He was outnumbered!

As the day fell into night, Ani-Man came in for a landing looking at his options. He was not going to be able to stop two hundred or more Polar Bears attacking the elves and Santa by himself. He needed to figure out a plan and by tomorrow but it might already be too late.

It was cold, even for an Eagle, especially now in the wintertime so close to Christmas. He decided to become a walrus for the night to help keep himself warm. It worked, and he was able to get a good night's rest, he would need it for tomorrow.

He began his day very early, with faint morning light. Quickly after a meal, he took to the air to survey how far Dark Zookeeper had moved his animals. It would be another two hundred miles to the North Pole. But with his transport planes, they would be there in just a few hours. Ani-Man became the Peregrine Falcon, the fastest bird in the world so he could keep up.

The transport plane after the flight began unloading its deadly cargo from up top of a hill, and within minutes, hundreds of hungry polar bears were ready to pounce into the toy factories and shipping departments below and put a stop to Christmas.

Time was running out. Would he call for help from Santa? It was too late. The bears formed an avalanche of strength and power and the poor little elves would be powerless to stop him.

Ani-Man had to think fast, he was never in such a situation before. First, he had to intercept them, so while in falcon form he dived hard until he was in front of them and returned back to his human form. But what he saw shocked him. So many powerful creatures thundering down on him. For the first time in his life, he was scared!

Thoughts raced through his mind at the speed of light! He could quickly turn back into a bird form and escape, but that would leave the North Pole destroyed. Quickly he could turn into a Polar Bear himself and growl trying to scare them back, but one against two hundred was not going to work. He could turn into a mighty lion, but no lion could live long here in the North Pole without freezing to death. He thought and thought...

He became more desperate and more desperate and then his body slowly started to transform. It started to become bigger. Slowly, he started to develop a very hard skin. Then slowly on his back, he started to develop wings! His face's jaw started changing and became a snout with huge teeth. He became even bigger, he kept growing and growing! Then he developed scales! He turned from a human skin color to white! And then the transformation was complete. Ani-Man had transformed into something he had never before become. He transformed into something he didn't even know he could become. Ani-man, after using his full concentration and all of his powers, became a White Dragon!

All the charging Polar Bears stopped in their tracks. They had never seen anything like that before! White Dragons live in the North Pole regions and breathe ice. He didn't want to hurt any of the bears so instead, he took a huge breath and breathed ice into each and every last one of them until they were frozen in place. And just like that, the disaster was averted. He had saved Christmas and was able to return all the bears to their natural homes, after destroying all the cages and making sure the Dark Zookeeper was locked up himself.

The elves never even knew the danger they were in, Ani-Man worked so quickly to restore the peace. No one actually knew what he had done, as no one visits the North Pole, you see. No one knew, except Santa.

When Christmas came, Ani-Man got one very special present straight from Santa himself. It was a statue of a Golden Dragon, made of real gold. The base had an inscription in it, "Thank you for saving Christmas, I always knew you had the heart of a Dragon, what you have done will never be forgotten.
-Santa"

The Annual Christmas Parade

You know, there are many many things that Santa loves and enjoys. There is practically not even anything related to Christmas that Santa doesn't absolutely love to death! Everything from Christmas ornaments, to the presents, to children being extra good, to seeing people's wonderful Christmas lights on their home, he absolutely loves seeing how people decorate their tree each year when he comes through the chimney, it's actually the first thing he looks at.

But there is one thing that he is not so interested in each year actually. As matter of fact, I would go so far as to say that he even dislikes it. Well, let's be real and honest for a second here and tell the full truth, Santa actually hates this thing. Of course, with Santa being Santa, he is such a kind-hearted fellow, he would never complain very much either so the fact that there is one thing that Santa actually hates is quite unknown to almost everyone in the world, except his closest elves and his wife. And that is the Annual Christmas parade.

You see, he doesn't actually dislike the parade itself, it is filled with a lot of energy and excitement each year, and he loves to see what floats they will come up with next. He wants to see how big the reindeer blow up dolls will be and will they have their own float, and all these things are absolutely awesome. There are many many parades all over the world leading up to Christmas and Santa loves every one of them. There is really only one problem. There are Christmas parades that occur on Christmas Day after all the presents have been opened and everyone is enjoying the day.

And by the time the parade is put on, Santa has usually been up for twenty-four hours delivering presents all over the world, has had more chocolate cookies and more milk, had flown through the coldest winds in a sleigh, had gone down millions of chimneys, that he is just utterly and completely and totally physically exhausted! He can barely stand.

And so for those few parades that he attends he pretty much has to load up on coffee beforehand to even stay awake through them at all. I mean imagine if you had to work super hard through the entire night helping all of mankind with your toy deliveries and then were asked to appear for all kinds of parades all around the world the very next day. Exhausting, right?

Normally, in those situations, Santa would like to use one of his very friendly and excellent body doubles that sometimes takes his place at malls every now and then, but he really hates not to be there for real because so many love to come out and enjoy themselves at the parade. I mean they come out there for him anyway, how could he not show up?

But if they were to look real closely, they might even find Santa nodding off and falling asleep during it. So Santa does whatever he can to make it through them, he doesn't want to disappoint anyone.

Santa was about ready to fly off to a parade in Spain when he stopped to talk to Mrs. Claus. "Oh, man! I don't think I can make it through this one honey. Do you think you could go in my place?" Mrs. Claus looked very concerned, "Oh no no no dear! All the children only want to see you, they don't want to see me. Come on why don't we just send one of your doubles, no one will ever really know the difference. You need to get some rest."

Santa was almost falling asleep when he said, "But the children want to see ME on this special day. Ok… Hey, do we have any stronger coffee that I could have maybe? There must be something we can do…"
Santa trailed off into sleep when a whole bunch of elves got together to carry him to the sleigh so he could make it to Spain on time.

He was sleeping the whole way there when the very loud music jogged him awake. He looked out at the huge gathered crowd in Madrid, the capital of Spain, and saw all the very excited children and began waving to them as best he could. Then he waved to the other side. He put up his best smile even though he was

practically ready to collapse. Maybe he needed some kind of powerful energy drink, thought Santa. Or, maybe he needed to just get some extra exercise, he was developing quite a belly after anyways. All those milk and cookies were not helping him get into better shape at all, no.

The energy of the music and the dancing and the bright eye of the young children kept him

interested, however.
And then it happened, Santa was waving to the children, when his arm fell and he collapsed into the chariot he was in!

The crowd gasped in horror! Was Santa all right!?
"Oh ho ho ho ho! Hello everybody." Santa quickly recovered, Why did they have to make these floats so comfortable! No one is able to stay awake in these things! There has to be some way to stay awake...

Then it occurred to him! He was in the float all alone, maybe if he had someone to talk to and keep him company, he would stay alert enough to make it through. Maybe Mrs. Clause could go with him to the next one.

Santa survived through and he had only twenty more parades to get through.

For the next one, Mrs. Claus was there with him the whole talking about what a wonderful job he had done. And she got some of the wonderful attention from the children as well. It was thrilling for her to be in front of so many cheering people.

And when Santa's arm fell down, Mrs. Claus propped it back up.

And when he got really sleepy, Mrs. Claus gave him some of his favorite eggnog to help keep him awake again.

And when there was something interesting to see or special someone in the crowd, Mrs. Claus pointed it out.

Over time, Santa learned that it was better to pre-record these parades on TV and then show them on Christmas Day so that more kids from around the world could see them at one time. If they were done before Christmas, Santa still had all the energy in the world.

And with Mrs. Claus by his Santa eventually grew to love parades again, and attended as many as possible. Maybe the next time you go to a parade, you will get a chance to see the real Santa. He never misses them.

Santa's Tips on How to Get onto the Good List

Today we are going to do something that is very special. We always have the idea that we need to be very good for Christmas, and the better we are the more gifts we will get from Santa right?

But what does being good really actually mean? Aren't we already good most of the time? Don't we already get most of what we want for Christmas?

Well, today we have a very special guest to answer some of these questions. We have none other than Santa Claus himself here to answer these questions and give some tips on how to maximize your Christmas to get everything you ever wished for.

Let's see what tips he has for us to learn from today, along with answering some questions from the children of the world.

Santa sat down on his large red chair with a big mailbag in front of him and gave some insight on Christmas we may never have known before.

"Ho ho ho! Well well, boys and girls. So you want to know how to be a good boy or girl do you?"

There was a group of children all sitting under him and they all nodded yes.

"You may be wondering, does being extra good actually help you get better presents? Do you want to know the answer to that?"

They nodded Yes!

"Well, the truth is, Yes, it does matter. But it doesn't just matter during Christmas time. When you treat others well and the way that you would want to be treated you will find that others will treat you very well too. It comes around back to you. If you are nice to others, you will find others will be nice to you. It is not just something to do during Christmas time, but all year. And the more you do it, the more you will find it will become easier for you. But I am definitely watching, and when someone is really good, the likelihood of excellent presents goes way way up for sure!"

The kids nodded in agreement, that made a lot of sense.

"Now you might wonder just how I keep track exactly if someone is being good or bad right? Did you know, with so many children in the world, I have to be highly organized and I actually have an exact system for doing that? Do you want to know what that is?"

Oh yes yes yes! All the kids became very excited and wanted to know.

"Well I put points next to each nice thing someone does and by December 24th, a child will usually have a score. The higher the number the better the child, the more presents they will get. Do you want to know what scores points?"

Oh yes yes yes! The children cheered and wanted to know.

"OK well it's very simple, saying please and thank you, or having good manners is 5 points. Doing your chores like dishes or laundry or making your bed, cleaning the inside of the car, sweeping, and helping to feed the pets are all 10 points each and every time that you do them. Do you want to know how you can score extra each time leading up to Christmas?"
Oh yes yes yes, How!?

"Well, if you make your parents, or sisters or brothers bed when they forget, or if someone forgets to do something and someone asks you to do it and you know how to do it and successfully do it then you score 20 points each time! Because you are working over and above your duties, that is always worth extra. But do you want to know how you can score even higher?"

Yes, yes yes!

"Well, when you are a little older, you can clean more and more and get bigger points! That's one of the reasons why growing up can be so exciting. Cleaning a whole bathroom, or kitchen or washing the car on the outside can be worth 30 to 50 points each time you do it! But do you want to know how to can get the MOST POINTS?"

Oh, YES YES YES, what is it?

"Well, to score the most points is to help around the house, WITHOUT anyone asking you to. If you ask your parents that you want to help learn how to contribute around the house by doing laundry or by changing the fish tank or any number of things, like packing your own lunch or emptying the dishwasher, without anyone asking you to do it, you gain 100 points! You just have to do it of your own free will, and not have anyone ask you to do it. That is what makes it the most special. Isn't that exciting!? That way I know you are growing up."
YES! YES! YES!

"Well, great boys and girls, I am looking forward to another wonderful year and with you choosing and deciding to help around the house only because YOU decided on it. And if you do that and keep it up, I can guarantee that it will be an amazing Christmas for you, because your friendliness and helpfulness will be rewarded by both your parents and myself. Now I can't wait to see what wonderful things you guys come up with. I will see you on Christmas and a wonderful year! Merry Christmas!"

And with that got up to a small cheering crowd of children and waved goodbye.

How do you like my bedtime stories?

I would really appreciate you leaving me a review.

Want my additional FREE BONUS PDF bedtime story book?

Like and contact me on my Facebook page:
https://www.facebook.com/Alex-Stone-109388640938614

or scan QR code to get to my Facebook Page:

or send me an email to get your free bonus PDF bedtime story book at:
alexstonebooks@gmail.com

Printed in the USA
CPSIA information can be obtained
at www.ICGtesting.com
LVHW081605111123
763517LV00007B/56

9 781087 918907